Eat Well Live Well

READER'S DIGEST

Light Bites and Lunches

Eat Well Live Well

READER'S DIGEST

Light Bites
and Lunches

Published by The Reader's Digest Association Limited
London • New York • Sydney • Montreal

LIGHT BITES AND LUNCHES is part of a series of cookery books called
EAT WELL LIVE WELL and was created by Amazon Publishing Limited.

Series Editor *Norma MacMillan*
Volume Editors *Maggie Pannell, Cécile Landau, Jane Middleton*
Art Director *Ruth Prentice*
Photographic Direction *Ruth Prentice*
DTP *Peter Howard*
Editorial Assistants *Jasmine Brown, Elizabeth Woodland*
Nutritionist *Jane Griffin, BSc (Nutri.), SRD,*

CONTRIBUTORS
Writers *Catherine Atkinson, Sara Buenfeld, Linda Collister, Christine France,
Bridget Jones, Janette Marshall, Maggie Pannell, Anne Sheasby*
Recipe Testers *Catherine Atkinson, Juliet Barker, Anna Brandenburger,
Anne Gains, Maggie Pannell, Anne Sheasby*
Photographers *Martin Brigdale, Gus Filgate, William Lingwood*
Stylist *Helen Trent*
Home Economists *Julie Beresford, Joanna Farrow, Bridget Sargeson,
Linda Tubby, Sunil Vijayakar*

FOR READER'S DIGEST
Project Editor *Rachel Warren Chadd*
Project Art Editor *Louise Turpin*
Production Controllers *Kathy Brown, Jane Holyer*

READER'S DIGEST GENERAL BOOKS
Editorial Director *Cortina Butler*
Art Director *Nick Clark*
Series Editor *Christine Noble*

ISBN 0 276 42475 1

First Edition Copyright © 2001
The Reader's Digest Association Limited
11 Westferry Circus, Canary Wharf, London E14 4HE
www.readersdigest.co.uk

Copyright © 2001 Reader's Digest Association Far East Limited
Philippines copyright © 2001 Reader's Digest Association Far East Limited

We are committed to both the quality of our products and the service we
provide to our customers. We value your comments, so please feel free to
contact us on 08705 113366, or by email at cust_service@readersdigest.co.uk
If you have any comments about the content of our books, you can contact us
at: gbeditorial@readersdigest.co.uk

Notes for the reader
• Use all metric or all imperial measures when preparing a recipe,
as the two sets of measurements are not exact equivalents.
• Recipes were tested using metric measures and conventional (not
fan-assisted) ovens. Medium eggs were used, unless otherwise
specified.
• Can sizes are approximate, as weights can vary slightly according
to the manufacturer.
• Preparation and cooking times are only intended as a guide.

The nutritional information in this book is for reference only.
The editors urge anyone with continuing medical problems or
symptoms to consult a doctor.

Contents

6
Introduction
Eating well to live well

8
A Lighter Way of Eating
10 Lighter eating in a healthy diet
12 A guide to good grazing
16 How to plan healthy lunches
18 Lunches to go
22 Celebration bites

26
Snacks, Nibbles and Dips
28 Tuscan bean crostini
30 Pitta crisps with hummus
32 Vegetable crisps with peanut dip
34 Tortilla chips with fresh mango and tomato salsa
36 Baked potato skins with smoked salmon and fresh dill
38 Spiced root vegetable wedges with creamy mustard dip
40 Piquant crab dip with crudités
42 Potato and courgette tortilla
44 Spiced fruits, nuts and seeds
46 Rosemary marinated olives

48
Tasty Bites
on Bread

50 Leek and ham pizza muffins
52 Chorizo, grilled pepper and tomato bruschetta
54 Hot and spicy tuna rolls
56 Mustard fried herring roes on Granary toast
58 Mushroom and thyme toasts
60 Cheese and onion rarebit
62 Sloppy Joes
64 Grilled salmon in ciabatta
66 Falafel pittas
68 Egg and anchovy pan bagna
70 Sardine, watercress and carrot open sandwich
72 Smoked trout wraps

74
Lunches for
All Occasions

76 Fennel and bean salad
78 Sugarsnap salad with black grapes and feta cheese
80 Middle Eastern salad
82 Tarragon chicken salad
84 Spiced couscous tomatoes
86 Salmon and tomato chowder
88 Japanese soup noodles with smoked tofu and bean sprouts
90 Mushroom and herb omelette
92 Stir-fry pork with Chinese greens
94 Home-style potato cakes with baked beef tomatoes
96 Smoked haddock hash
98 Chicken and cashew pancakes
100 Thai coconut rice with prawns
102 Baked rigatoni with aubergine
104 Cheese and watercress soufflé
106 Lentil risotto

108
Special
Bites

110 Monkfish and mussel sticks
112 Gingered crab filo parcels
114 Sticky spare ribs
116 Caramelised onion tartlets
118 Smoked turkey and apricot bites
120 Fish dim sum
122 Stuffed mushrooms
124 Pissaladière
126 Chicken yakitori
128 Goat's cheese toasts
130 Sushi rolls
132 Greek meatballs with lemon dip
134 Sesame cheese twists

136
Sweet
Treats

138 Orange and pecan biscuits
140 Caramelised banana crumpets
142 Apple and hazelnut drop scones
144 Date and walnut flapjacks
146 Summer berry muffins
148 Sticky prune and ginger teabread
150 Fruit and pistachio baklava
152 Fruit brochettes with rosewater cashew cream
154 Mango smoothie

156 A glossary of nutritional terms
159 Index

Eating well to live well

Eating a healthy diet can help you look good, feel great and have lots of energy. Nutrition fads come and go, but the simple keys to eating well remain the same: enjoy a variety of food – no single food contains all the vitamins, minerals, fibre and other essential components you need for health and vitality – and get the balance right by looking at the proportions of the different foods you eat. Add some regular exercise too – at least 30 minutes a day, 3 times a week – and you'll be helping yourself to live well and make the most of your true potential.

Getting it into proportion

Current guidelines are that most people in the UK should eat more starchy foods, more fruit and vegetables, and less fat, meat products and sugary foods. It is almost impossible to give exact amounts that you should eat, as every single person's requirements vary, depending on size, age and the amount of energy expended during the day. However, nutrition experts have suggested an ideal balance of the different foods that provide us with energy (calories) and the nutrients needed for health. The number of daily portions of each of the food groups will vary from person to person – for example, an active teenager might need to eat up to 14 portions of starchy carbohydrates every day, whereas a sedentary adult would only require 6 or 7 portions – but the proportions of the food groups in relation to each other should ideally stay the same.

More detailed explanations of food groups and nutritional terms can be found on pages 156–158, together with brief guidelines on amounts which can be used in conjunction with the nutritional analyses of the recipes. A simple way to get the balance right, however, is to imagine a daily 'plate' divided into the different food groups. On the imaginary 'plate', starchy carbohydrates fill at least one-third of the space, thus constituting the main part of your meals. Fruit and vegetables fill the same amount of space. The remaining third of the 'plate' is divided mainly between protein foods and dairy foods, with just a little space allowed for foods containing fat and sugar. These are the proportions to aim for.

It isn't essential to eat the ideal proportions on the 'plate' at every meal, or even every day – balancing them over a week or two is just as good. The healthiest diet for you and your family is one that is generally balanced and sustainable in the long term.

Our daily plate

Starchy carbohydrate foods: eat 6–14 portions a day
At least 50% of the calories in a healthy diet should come from carbohydrates, and most of that from starchy foods – bread, potatoes and other starchy vegetables, pasta, rice and cereals. For most people in the UK this means doubling current intake. Starchy carbohydrates are the best foods for energy. They also provide protein and essential vitamins and minerals, particularly those from the B group. Eat a variety of starchy foods, choosing wholemeal or wholegrain types whenever possible, because the fibre they contain helps to prevent constipation, bowel disease, heart disease and other health problems.
What is a portion of starchy foods?
Some examples are: 3 tbsp breakfast cereal • 2 tbsp muesli • 1 slice of bread or toast • 1 bread roll, bap or bun • 1 small pitta bread, naan bread or chapatti • 3 crackers or crispbreads • 1 medium-sized potato • 1 medium-sized plantain or small sweet potato • 2 heaped tbsp boiled rice • 2 heaped tbsp boiled pasta.

Fruit and vegetables: eat at least 5 portions a day
Nutrition experts are unanimous that we would all benefit from eating more fruit and vegetables each day – a total of at least 400 g (14 oz) of fruit and vegetables (edible part) is the target. Fruit and vegetables provide vitamin C for immunity and healing, and other 'antioxidant' vitamins and minerals for protection against cardiovascular disease and cancer. They also offer several 'phytochemicals' that help protect against cancer, and B vitamins, especially folate, which is important for women planning a pregnancy, to prevent birth defects. All of these, plus other nutrients, work together to boost well-being.

Antioxidant nutrients (e.g. vitamins C and beta-carotene, which are mainly derived from fruit and vegetables) and vitamin E help to prevent harmful free radicals in the body initiating or accelerating cancer, heart disease, cataracts, arthritis, general ageing, sun damage to skin, and damage to sperm. Free radicals occur naturally as a by-product of normal cell function, but are also caused by pollutants such as tobacco smoke and over-exposure to sunlight.
What is a portion of fruit or vegetables?
Some examples are: 1 medium-sized portion of vegetables or salad • 1 medium-sized piece of fresh fruit • 6 tbsp (about 140 g/5 oz) stewed or canned fruit • 1 small glass (100 ml/3½ fl oz) fruit juice.

Dairy foods: eat 2–3 portions a day
Dairy foods, such as milk, cheese, yogurt and fromage frais, are the best source of calcium for strong bones and teeth, and important for the nervous system. They also provide some protein for growth and repair, vitamin B_{12}, and vitamin A for healthy eyes. They are particularly valuable foods for young children, who need full-fat versions at least up to age 2. Dairy foods are also especially important for adolescent girls to prevent the development of osteoporosis later in life, and for women throughout life generally.

To limit fat intake, wherever possible adults should choose lower-fat dairy foods, such as semi-skimmed milk and low-fat yogurt.
What is a portion of dairy foods?
Some examples are: 1 medium-sized glass (200 ml/7 fl oz) milk • 1 matchbox-sized piece (40 g/1½ oz) Cheddar cheese • 1 small pot of yogurt • 125 g (4½ oz) cottage cheese or fromage frais.

Protein foods: eat 2–4 portions a day

Lean meat, fish, eggs and vegetarian alternatives provide protein for growth and cell repair, as well as iron to prevent anaemia. Meat also provides B vitamins for healthy nerves and digestion, especially vitamin B_{12}, and zinc for growth and healthy bones and skin. Only moderate amounts of these protein-rich foods are required. An adult woman needs about 45 g of protein a day and an adult man 55 g, which constitutes about 11% of a day's calories. This is less than the current average intake. For optimum health, we need to eat some protein every day.

What is a portion of protein-rich food?

Some examples are: 3 slices (85–100 g/3–3½ oz) of roast beef, pork, ham, lamb or chicken • about 100 g (3½ oz) grilled offal • 115–140 g (4–5 oz) cooked fillet of white or oily fish (not fried in batter) • 3 fish fingers • 2 eggs (up to 7 a week) • about 140 g/5 oz baked beans • 60 g (2¼ oz) nuts, peanut butter or other nut products.

Foods containing fat: 1–5 portions a day

Unlike fruit, vegetables and starchy carbohydrates, which can be eaten in abundance, fatty foods should not exceed 33% of the day's calories in a balanced diet, and only 10% of this should be from saturated fat. This quantity of fat may seem a lot, but it isn't – fat contains more than twice as many calories per gram as either carbohydrate or protein.

Overconsumption of fat is a major cause of weight and health problems. A healthy diet must contain a certain amount of fat to provide fat-soluble vitamins and essential fatty acids, needed for the development and function of the brain, eyes and nervous system, but we only need a small amount each day – just 25 g is required, which is much less than we consume in our Western diet. The current recommendations from the Department of Health are a maximum of 71 g fat (of this, 21.5 g saturated) for women each day and 93.5 g fat (28.5 g saturated) for men. The best sources of the essential fatty acids are natural fish oils and pure vegetable oils.

What is a portion of fatty foods?

Some examples are: 1 tsp butter or margarine • 2 tsp low-fat spread • 1 tsp cooking oil • 1 tbsp mayonnaise or vinaigrette (salad dressing) • 1 tbsp cream • 1 individual packet of crisps.

Foods containing sugar: 0–2 portions a day

Although many foods naturally contain sugars (e.g. fruit contains fructose, milk lactose), health experts recommend that we limit 'added' sugars. Added sugars, such as table sugar, provide only calories – they contain no vitamins, minerals or fibre to contribute to health, and it is not necessary to eat them at all. But, as the old adage goes, 'a little of what you fancy does you good' and sugar is no exception. Denial of foods, or using them as rewards or punishment, is not a healthy attitude to eating, and can lead to cravings, binges and yo-yo dieting. Sweet foods are a pleasurable part of a well-balanced diet, but added sugars should account for no more than 11% of the total daily carbohydrate intake.

In assessing how much sugar you consume, don't forget that it is a major ingredient of many processed and ready-prepared foods.

What is a portion of sugary foods?

Some examples are: 3 tsp sugar • 1 heaped tsp jam or honey • 2 biscuits • half a slice of cake • 1 doughnut • 1 Danish pastry • 1 small bar of chocolate • 1 small tube or bag of sweets.

Too salty

Salt (sodium chloride) is essential for a variety of body functions, but we tend to eat too much through consumption of salty processed foods, 'fast' foods and ready-prepared foods, and by adding salt in cooking and at the table. The end result can be rising blood pressure as we get older, which puts us at higher risk of heart disease and stroke. Eating more vegetables and fruit increases potassium intake, which can help to counteract the damaging effects of salt.

Alcohol in a healthy diet

In recent research, moderate drinking of alcohol has been linked with a reduced risk of heart disease and stroke among men and women over 45. However, because of other risks associated with alcohol, particularly in excessive quantities, no doctor would recommend taking up drinking if you are teetotal. The healthiest pattern of drinking is to enjoy small amounts of alcohol with food, to have alcohol-free days and always to avoid getting drunk. A well-balanced diet is vital because nutrients from food (vitamins and minerals) are needed to detoxify the alcohol.

Water – the best choice

Drinking plenty of non-alcoholic liquid each day is an often overlooked part of a well-balanced diet. A minimum of 8 glasses (which is about 2 litres/3½ pints) is the ideal. If possible, these should not all be tea or coffee, as these are stimulants and diuretics, which cause the body to lose liquids, taking with them water-soluble vitamins. Water is the best choice. Other good choices are fruit or herb teas or tisanes, fruit juices – diluted with water, if preferred – or semi-skimmed milk (full-fat milk for very young children). Fizzy sugary or acidic drinks such as cola are more likely to damage tooth enamel than other drinks.

As a guide to the vitamin and mineral content of foods and recipes in the book, we have used the following terms and symbols, based on the percentage of the daily RNI provided by one serving for the average adult man or woman aged 19–49 years (see also pages 156–158):

✓✓✓ *or* excellent   at least 50% (half)

✓✓ *or* good   25–50% (one-quarter to one-half)

✓ *or* useful   10–25% (one-tenth to one-quarter)

Note that recipes contribute other nutrients, but the analyses only include those that provide at least 10% RNI per portion. Vitamins and minerals where deficiencies are rare are not included.

Ⓥ denotes that a recipe is suitable for vegetarians.

A Lighter Way
of Eating

Little and often for health and energy

ALL OVER THE WORLD, IN ALL CULTURES and cuisines, there are tempting snacks to satisfy the urge to nibble, as well as lighter meals to enjoy in the middle of the day. Here, in our multicultural society, we have a great variety of deliciously different bites and lunches available to us, and we can choose to eat little and often if that suits our modern lifestyles. This can be just as healthy as the traditional 3 meals a day, as long as the foods we eat are varied and nutritious, and our overall diet is well-balanced. What we eat is much more important than when.

Lighter eating in a healthy diet

Although many people still like to have 3 full meals a day, others are choosing a lighter way of eating – either occasionally or as a lifestyle change – consisting of a series of snacks rather than substantial meals. Either option is equally valid. The important thing is to make sure your overall diet is healthy and well-balanced.

Eating to suit your lifestyle

The demands of modern life mean that we don't always have the opportunity to sit down and eat 3 meals a day. For some people, the pressures of combining work and family leave little time for food preparation. Others regularly eat on their own and don't want to bother cooking a full meal. Even in families, individuals may all have different schedules.

With the advent of the microwave and freezer, and the boom in cook-chill meals and convenience foods, it's much easier now to eat little and often, eating what we want when we want it. And the range of foods to snack on is vast, with so much on offer from other countries' cuisines. But to eat well it's important to choose the right foods and ensure that we don't miss out nutritionally when we're not following a traditional meal structure.

Little and often

There is no 'right' way of eating, as long as you take in all the nutrients your body requires. The really important thing is what you eat, not when. If you prefer to snack sometimes, try to choose foods that are appropriate to your calorie needs and to balance the foods you eat throughout the day, making sure you have an adequate intake from the main food groups: starchy carbohydrates, fruit and vegetables, and protein foods.

Eating little and often can be beneficial for health, as it helps to maintain blood sugar levels. However, there can be a danger of eating too much – of little and often becoming lots and often! We don't eat only because we're hungry. Boredom or stress can drive us to the fridge, canteen or corner shop, and without a traditional meal structure to guide us it can be hard to keep track of how much we're consuming. If you make sure all your snacks are nutritious ones, as well as lower in fat and sugar, you are less likely to eat beyond your body's needs.

What is a healthy snack?

It's tempting to turn to sweet biscuits, chocolate confectionery and crisps when you want a snack. While it won't do any harm to enjoy these foods occasionally, if they become a regular part of the diet, your intake of saturated fat will increase and you may go short of vital nutrients. A healthy snack, on the other hand, can make a significant contribution of vitamins and minerals, dietary fibre and essential fats (as opposed to saturated fats).

Starchy carbohydrates, such as bread, cereals, potatoes, rice and pasta, have a lot to offer nutritionally and make excellent choices as the basis both for snacks and for lunch. They are filling without being high in calories, and help to keep you topped up with energy and on an even keel throughout the day.

Fresh fruit is a good choice for a light snack. Although not as filling as starchy carbohydrate foods, many fruits are high in disease-fighting antioxidants such as vitamins C and E, and beta-carotene.

Making time for lunch

No matter what our eating pattern is for the rest of the day, most of us do try to make time for lunch of some sort, even if it is just a 'light bite' – a sandwich in the office, a simple hot dish or salad in the canteen, or a quick bowl of soup at home. Lunch is an essential pause in the middle of the day, a chance to relax and recharge our batteries a little.

In the office it's all too easy to rush out and grab some processed fast food, or at home to reach for a can or packet, but these may not offer the best way to boost flagging energy levels. It only takes a little advance preparation and not much effort to make sure your lunch is full of good things that will increase your intake of nutrients and provide the energy to keep you going all through the afternoon.

a lighter way of eating

► Nibbling Spiced fruits, nuts and seeds (see page 44) is a great way to keep hunger pangs at bay

▼ Egg and anchovy pan bagna (see page 68) makes a well-balanced and satisfying picnic lunch

▲ Tarragon chicken salad (see page 82) is a delicious, nutritious dish to prepare for lunch at home

◄ Tortilla chips with fresh mango and tomato salsa (see page 34) can provide a quick energy boost after school or exercise

a lighter way of eating

A guide to good grazing

By making sure your choice of foods is varied and well balanced, you can enjoy frequent snacks throughout the day that will optimise your energy levels and promote good health without encouraging weight problems.

Watching what you eat

Snacks and little nibbles can make a nutritious contribution to your diet, no matter when they are eaten. It's important, though, to try to make the best choices and to avoid too frequent nibbling, as this can lead to weight problems.

Most children need something to eat when they come in from school. Adults, too, often want a snack in a busy day. With a little forward planning to keep the fridge and storecupboard stocked with healthy snack foods, you can make sure that your snacks are nutritious. When you need to replace energy quickly, a snack that scores high or moderate on the Glycaemic Index (see page 15) is the answer, but if you want a slow release of energy, to sustain you over a longer period, low-GI foods are a better choice.

Healthy fridge fodder

If you often find yourself heading for the fridge when you're hungry, keep healthy snack foods such as these to tempt you.

- Hummus, salsas and yogurt-based dips – preferably home-made (see pages 30, 34 and 38). These can provide a variety of nutrients, including protein (chickpeas in hummus), vitamin C (fruit and vegetables in salsa) and calcium (in yogurt).
- Vegetable crudités, such as strips of red pepper, sticks of carrot, celery and cucumber, broccoli florets and cherry tomatoes, packed in sealed polythene bags (they'll keep for 1–2 days). Raw vegetables contain the antioxidants vitamin C and beta-carotene, as well as dietary fibre and a variety of phytochemicals.
- Cheese, which is a good source of protein and calcium. Soft cheeses, preferably those lower in fat such as fromage frais, quark or ricotta, can be spread on bread or crispbreads.
- Lean cooked meats such as chicken, turkey and ham, which provide protein and B vitamins.
- Smoked fish such as salmon and trout, or fish pâtés based on tuna or smoked mackerel. Oily fish is a rich source of the essential omega-3 fatty acids.

Keep your fridge stocked with nutritious snack foods, such as vegetables to cut for crudités; berries, plums, grapes and other soft fruits; thinly sliced lean cooked meats; and dairy products such as cheese and yogurt

- Fresh soup made with lots of vegetables. Soup retains the water-soluble nutrients of the ingredients used.
- Plain low-fat yogurt, which can be mixed with fresh or dried fruit or muesli, or sweetened with a little fruit purée or honey. Yogurt contains beneficial bacteria for a healthy digestion and immune system.
- Soft fruits such as berries, grapes, cherries, plums and peaches. These provide antioxidants and potassium.

Simple storecupboard snacks

Instead of opening a bag of crisps, try one of these tasty ideas using nutritious foods in jars and packets.
- Tapenade, a paste made from black olives, spread on bread, rice cakes or oatcakes. Olives and olive oil contain vitamin E and healthy monounsaturated fatty acids.
- Unsweetened or low-sugar muesli, with semi-skimmed milk. Cereals such as muesli offer high-fibre starchy carbohydrate, and you get protein and calcium from the milk.
- Nuts and seeds, preferably unsalted. Nuts provide protein, and both nuts and seeds are rich in many nutrients – vitamins, minerals, fibre and essential fatty acids (omega-3 from nuts and omega-6 from seeds).
- Breadsticks, rice cakes and oatcakes, either eaten plain or with a spread, salsa or dip. Like bread, these are good sources of starchy carbohydrate and dietary fibre.
- Dried fruit, such as a few dates, raisins, apricots or prunes.

The storecupboard can be a good source of healthy snacks, such as nuts and seeds; oatcakes; dried fruits; muesli; breadsticks; breads of all kinds; and oatcakes

These are high in dietary fibre and a useful source of minerals such as iron and potassium as well as being a great source of energy. Note, though, that they are high in calories too, so can spoil small appetites if eaten in large quantities.

After-school snacks

When children come in from school claiming that they're 'starving', offer them one of these satisfying snacks.
- Fresh fruit such as an apple (good for teeth and gums), a banana (a better source of energy than refined sugary foods) or a few juicy pineapple wedges (good source of vitamin C), or a small handful of energy-boosting dried fruit.
- Bread, which is a good source of starchy carbohydrate, fibre, B vitamins, iron and calcium. Spread toasted or fresh slices of wholemeal or mixed grain bread with peanut butter, soft cheese or jam. Or fill mini pitta breads and bagels with a little canned fish or hard-boiled egg and salad.
- Cheese in small cubes or slices, with tomatoes or fresh fruit. Cheese is a good source of protein, calcium and vitamin B_{12}.
- A teacake or slice of teabread, preferably home-baked. These are a nutritious sweet alternative to confectionery, offering more than sugar alone.
- A biscuit or flapjack, preferably home-baked. Home-made baked goods are usually lower in fat and sugar than bought ones, and don't contain additives.
- A milk shake or smoothie made with fresh fruit.

Drinks are an important part of healthy lunches and snacks, and many contain essential nutrients. Fresh fruit smoothies make a satisfying quick snack; fruit and vegetable juices are deliciously refreshing; a hot milky drink at bedtime is relaxing; and fruit and herb teas make an invigorating alternative to coffee

Quick energy boosts after exercise

If you exercise regularly, it is important to re-stock your stores of muscle glycogen as soon as possible after your exercise or training session finishes. High and moderate GI foods are the best choices. Here are some delicious ideas.

- Bagel with low-fat soft cheese and jam.
- Toast or crumpet with jam.
- Baked jacket potato topped with a fresh salsa.
- Small handful of raisins.
- Muesli bar.
- Thick vegetable soup with bread roll.
- Muffin, preferably home-baked and low in fat.

Full-of-goodness drinks

Drinks can make an important contribution to a healthy diet, and some of them are filling enough to serve as a snack.

- Fruit and vegetable juices, which supply vitamins and minerals. If you drink them frequently, it's best to dilute them with water.

- Milk, preferably semi-skimmed. Although it will have less of the fat-soluble vitamins A, D and E, semi-skimmed milk is a good source of protein and calcium. Note though that children under 5 should always have full-fat milk.
- Milk shakes and smoothies, made by puréeing ripe fresh fruit in a blender with milk, yogurt or fruit juice, sometimes with the addition of ice-cream or frozen yogurt. These frothy drinks contribute protein and calcium from the milk, plus vitamins from the fruit, and are a good way of masking milk for those who don't like its taste.
- Herb, green and fruit teas, which offer a variety of possible medicinal and therapeutic benefits.

Bedtime snacks

Although it's best not to eat a heavy meal late in the evening, some people do like to have a little snack before they go to bed. In this case, it makes sense to choose one that is high in carbohydrates, such as bread, cereal, rice or bananas. These increase the brain's uptake of the amino acid, tryptophan, which is needed to make serotonin, a natural sedative. Milk also contains tryptophan, so there is some sense in the old idea of a hot milky drink to help you sleep.

Food for longer-lasting energy

The Glycaemic Index (GI) ranks foods based on the rate that they raise blood sugar levels, so it can be useful for planning healthy snacks. Foods with a high GI factor cause a rapid rise in blood sugar levels, giving a quick energy boost, whereas those with a low GI factor cause a slow, steady rise and offer longer-term, sustained energy. People used to believe that for quick energy, sugars were digested and absorbed more rapidly than starchy carbohydrates, but it is not always easy to predict which foods are best for that, as the table below shows. Many things can affect the GI factor of a food, including its physical characteristics, its fibre, sugar, fat and protein content, and other foods eaten at the same time.

	LOW GI	MODERATE GI	HIGH GI
Bread, biscuits and cake	chapattis, Granary and multigrain bread, pitta bread, rye bread, fruit loaf, sponge cake, banana cake	crispbread, oatcakes, digestive biscuits, flapjacks, muesli bars, muffins	bagels, baguettes, brown, white and wholemeal bread, water biscuits, rice cakes
Breakfast cereals	100% bran cereal, muesli, oat and wheat flakes, porridge, crunchy rice and wheat flakes, sultana bran	100% whole wheat cereal, crunchy wheat and malted barley cereal, toasted wholegrain cereal	cornflakes, crispy rice cereal, whole wheat biscuits, puffed rice and wheat cereals
Dairy products	low-fat ice-cream, milk, yogurt, frozen yogurt	full-fat ice-cream	
Drinks	fruit juices, sugar-free drinks	cola, sports drinks	glucose drinks
Fruit, vegetables and nuts	apples, dried apricots, bananas, grapefruit, grapes, kiwi fruit, mango, oranges, peaches, pears, plums, carrots, peas, sweetcorn, peanuts	papaya, pineapple, raisins, sultanas, butternut squash	watermelon, broad beans, parsnips, pumpkin, swede
Potatoes, rice and pasta	crisps, sweet potatoes, basmati rice, noodles, most types of pasta	boiled potatoes, new potatoes, macaroni	chips, jacket baked potatoes, mashed potatoes, brown and white rice
Pulses and grains	baked beans, chickpeas, dried beans (black-eyed, butter, haricot, kidney, soya), kasha (buckwheat), lentils, pearl barley, popcorn, bulghur wheat	cornmeal/polenta, couscous, millet taco shells	corn chips, tapioca
Sugars	fructose (from fruit and vegetables), lactose (from milk), most chocolate	honey, sucrose (table sugar), some chocolate bars	glucose

How to plan healthy lunches

Whether you take a packed lunch to work or school or buy a sandwich, or eat at home or in a local cafe or restaurant, deciding what to have for lunch can be a dilemma. Here's how to make the healthiest choices.

Balancing lunch with the rest of the day's meals

If you keep in mind what you have eaten and will be eating during the rest of the day, you can plan your lunch in the context of your overall diet. For example, if you had a good, nourishing breakfast, a simple sandwich or salad will probably be sufficient for lunch. If you skipped breakfast (see Breakfast on the move, page 20, for future reference), it's a good idea to have a more substantial lunch that includes lots of starchy carbohydrates, fruit and vegetables and some protein-rich food. If you have a sustaining meal like this at lunchtime, then a fairly simple evening meal will do, such as a salad or soup with bread, a light rice or pasta dish, or a vegetable dish such as a stir-fry or gratin.

We can't always control what we eat for lunch – for example, if it is provided for us – and it may not always be as nutritious as we would like. In this case, snacks are an ideal way to boost intake of vitamins and minerals, with fruit, both fresh and dried, vegetables (e.g. crudités with a light dip), nuts and seeds, and dairy products such as yogurt and milk.

Does it have to be cooked to count?

While it is true that hot food seems more satisfying and filling than cold, the idea that hot food alone equals a 'proper meal' is a myth. As long as a dish is nutritious and part of a varied, well-balanced diet, it doesn't matter whether the food is hot or cold, or even if it is cooked or raw.

If you do prefer hot food at lunchtime, it doesn't have to be a large, heavy meal. A nourishing soup, simple risotto, light pasta dish, omelette, stir-fry or a salad with a hot component such as a jacket baked potato can all be satisfying without being heavy and high in fat, which has the effect of slowing you down for the rest of the day rather than re-energising you. Hot sandwiches are also excellent at lunchtime (see pages 52–66 for some tasty ideas).

Guidelines for a healthy lunch

The ideal lunch should offer something from all the major food groups, in varying proportions. Try to include the following:
- A good helping of starchy carbohydrate, such as bread, pasta, potatoes, and rice or other grains.
- Lots of vegetables and fruit.
- A moderate amount of protein-rich food, such as meat, fish, nuts, cheese and eggs.
- A little fat, such as vegetable or nut oil (e.g. sunflower and extra virgin olive oils).

This might sound like a lot to think about, but in practice most simple lunches can meet all these guidelines, and the meal need not be large and filling. Here are some examples of healthy lunches: a sandwich filled with roasted vegetables and mozzarella cheese, or chicken and lightly dressed salad, followed by an apple or other piece of fresh fruit and yogurt; a baked jacket potato with a sprinkling of grated Cheddar cheese, a watercress and orange salad, and a fresh fruit smoothie; a mixed vegetable and nut or meat stir-fry with rice or noodles, followed by a banana and a few dates; a bowl of hearty fish or chicken and vegetable chowder with bread rolls, followed by fromage frais and fresh berries.

Take a break, have a lunch hour

Stopping work, study or chores in the middle of the day to eat lunch sometimes seems like a waste of time, but it's vital to recharge your batteries. Allowing yourself a pause, with time to eat a nourishing lunch without rushing, reduces the risk of digestive problems and helps to combat stress. Even better is if you can also fit in a short walk and a breath of fresh air, which will help to reinvigorate the mind and body, so you are refreshed and ready to start the afternoon's activities.

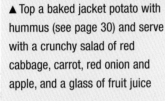

▲ Top a baked jacket potato with hummus (see page 30) and serve with a crunchy salad of red cabbage, carrot, red onion and apple, and a glass of fruit juice

◀ Enjoy a bowl of Salmon and tomato chowder (see page 86) with plenty of bread, fruit and vegetable crudités, and a Date and walnut flapjack (see page 144)

▼ Try a square of Pissaladière (see page 124; add some mozzarella before baking) with a green leaf and vegetable salad, fresh fruit such as grapes and a glass of wine

Strategies for business lunches

If business lunches are a rare treat for you, they will not have a great impact on your day-to-day eating. However, if they are a regular feature of your lifestyle, you need a strategy to ensure they do not upset the balance of your diet, increasing your intake of saturated fats and possibly causing weight gain.

One idea is to eat in restaurants and cafes where you are likely to find some healthier choices on the menu, such as ethnic restaurants. Another good idea is to go where you can eat as much or as little as you want. Modern brasseries, where there is a less formal meal structure, fit this option, as you can choose 2 starters instead of a starter and a main dish if you prefer a light meal.

Here are a few examples of restaurant cuisines that usually offer some healthy dishes on the menu, with advice on the best choices.

Chinese/Thai Choose steamed rather than deep-fried foods (the steamed dumplings called dim sum are varied and delicious for lunch), plus clear broth-based soups, noodle dishes, plain rice (not fried) and stir-fries.

Fusion food This mixes classic French and British dishes with Oriental ingredients and techniques. There will usually be some imaginative vegetable dishes and grilled meat, poultry and fish on offer. Go for those with Oriental-style sauces and garnishes, which are generally lower in fat than Western ones.

Greek/Middle Eastern This is perfect for people who like to nibble at lunchtime – ask for a mezze, which is a selection of little dishes that several people can share. Usually the portions are small and there are plenty of vegetables, breads and dips made with pulses. A more substantial choice is a Middle Eastern couscous-based dish.

Indian Tandoori dishes and kebabs are good choices, as they are baked and won't be laden with high-fat ghee. Have them with naan breads or plain rice and cucumber raita.

Italian and Mediterranean Try grilled vegetables as a light starter, or a fish soup, and choose pasta, meat or fish dishes with a vegetable or tomato sauce rather than a rich, creamy one. Risotto is another good choice.

Japanese Japanese restaurants tend to offer light dishes that are low in fat, as long as you avoid deep-fried foods such as tempura. Good choices are chicken and noodles in miso soup, sukiyaki, sushi and teriyaki.

Lunches to go

Try to make packed lunches not only nutritious but colourful and fun to eat – suitable for public scrutiny (or peer group pressure in the case of children) and as original and varied as possible. A tall order? No, read this...

Travelling light

Sandwiches may be the ultimate portable meal, but there are plenty of other options that are easy to pack in a lunchbox and just as satisfying to eat. When planning a packed lunch, choose foods that will travel well, and include a drink, preferably something simple such as water or fruit juice, unless you can buy this. Don't forget to include a fork and spoon, if necessary, plus a handwipe or paper napkin.

It's important to observe good hygiene when preparing packed lunches, particularly for children. Cut food on a clean board with clean knives, and keep all foods well chilled before packing, especially those that are susceptible to food poisoning bacteria (e.g. meat, fish, eggs, poultry and dairy products). If preparing a packed lunch the night before, wrap it well and store it in the fridge. In hot weather, pack the meal in an insulated box or bag with an ice pack.

Super sandwiches

It's amazing what you can pack between 2 slices of bread, and how nourishing and satisfying a sandwich can be. Whether you make your own or buy it, there is an endless variety of breads and sandwich fillings to choose from.

Tips for successful and healthy sandwiches

- If buttering the bread, soften the butter first so it is easier to spread thinly and sparingly.
- To prevent soggy sandwiches, rather than buttering the bread, put some lettuce leaves between the filling and the bread.
- To add extra flavour and moisture, instead of butter or mayonnaise, try a sprinkling of balsamic vinegar, soy sauce or lemon juice, or spread the bread with a salsa or fruity chutney.

In sandwich bars, where sandwiches are made to order, it's easy to specify exactly what you want. In shops that sell prepacked sandwiches your options will be more limited. Here's how to make healthy choices.

- In sandwich bars, avoid fillings that are swimming in dressing, which are often high in fat. Stipulate whether or not you want anything spread on the bread.

▲ Mix canned crab meat with lemon juice, Dijon mustard and Tabasco sauce to taste and put between thick slices of wholemeal bread with sliced cucumber and frisée

▼ Fill ciabatta bread or rolls with wafer-thin slices of smoked ham, sliced tomatoes and red onion, and shavings of Parmesan cheese

a lighter way of eating

- Try to avoid sandwiches made with mayonnaise, which is normally slathered on the bread far more thickly than you would at home.
- Choose thick sliced bread rather than thin, or chunky breads such as ciabatta, baguette and focaccia.
- When buying prepacked sandwiches, look for a fresh appearance and always check the use-by date on the pack.
- Read the label on sandwiches labelled low-fat or low-calorie as they can sometimes be low in nutrients too. Use the ingredients list to assess how healthy the sandwich is.

Tasty filling ideas

Sandwiches can make a great receptacle for leftovers, such as roast or grilled meat or poultry, poached fish, grilled vegetables and so on, or you can use storecupboard standbys such as canned fish and vegetables. The ideas below are just a few of the myriad fillings for nutritious sandwiches.

- Canned tuna (in spring water), canned sweetcorn kernels, green olives or capers, and low-fat soft cheese, plus crunchy leaves such as cos or Little Gem lettuce.
- Sliced or mashed avocado and smoked salmon or trout (or cottage cheese) sprinkled with lime juice and black pepper, plus watercress or Oak Leaf lettuce leaves.
- Tapenade (black olive pâté), sliced hard-boiled egg and watercress.
- Lean Parma ham, sliced ripe figs and rocket.
- Crumbled blue cheese, baby spinach leaves and pecan nuts.
- Canned sardines, shaved fennel and fresh basil leaves.
- Hummus, halved cherry tomatoes, strips of red pepper and shredded Chinese leaves (wrapped up in soft flour tortillas).
- Griddled Mediterranean vegetables (courgette, aubergine, onion and peppers) with balsamic vinegar and rocket.
- Canned chickpeas mashed with tahini dressing, black olives and grated carrot, plus mixed salad leaves (best in pitta bread).
- Slices of chicken breast, minted yogurt, fresh mango and soft lettuce leaves.
- Peanut butter, low-fat soft cheese and grated carrot (this is a favourite with children).
- Canned salmon mixed with plain low-fat yogurt and a little mayonnaise, topped with thin cucumber slices.
- Diced chicken and canned sweetcorn kernels bound with a little lemon mayonnaise, plus mustard and cress.

▲ Blend ricotta cheese with grated apple and carrot, plus lemon or orange juice to taste, and spread between slices of oatmeal or multigrain bread

▼ Toss cooked peeled prawns with a little mayonnaise and tomato ketchup and wrap in flour tortillas with shredded iceberg lettuce

Beyond the white sliced loaf

Bread is such a fundamental part of our diet that it's easy to take it for granted and forget what a wonderful source of nourishment it is. Eating several slices of good-quality bread a day is an easy way of obtaining a high proportion of our daily supply of energy and vitamins – especially the important B vitamin group, which helps to regulate the nervous system, converts food into energy and performs many more tasks. Most breads also contain iron, calcium and other nutrients, are low in fat and a good source of starchy carbohydrates. Speciality breads can provide extra nutrients by including ingredients such as fruits, olives, nuts and seeds.

a lighter way of eating

Breakfast on the move ...

Breakfast replenishes energy levels after the night 'fast', and people who eat breakfast regularly perform better at work or school, have fewer mood swings and are less likely to have weight problems. If you don't have time for breakfast before you set out in the morning, try taking one of the following with you.

• 2 slices of lightly buttered cinnamon raisin bread or a thick slice of fruited teabread, plus a couple of clementines or an orange.

• Oatcakes sandwiched together with a little honey, plus a banana or a tub of fresh berries.

• An individual portion of unsweetened muesli or granola, plus a small carton of milk or a pot of plain low-fat yogurt to mix with it.

• A tub of ricotta cheese and a few ripe apricots.

• A handful of mixed dried fruit and seeds/nuts.

• A tub of fruit salad, a pot of plain low-fat yogurt, and a home-made muffin, flapjack or fruit scone (see Date and walnut flapjacks, page 144 and Summer berry muffins, page 146).

▲ For a home-made packed lunch, make Mediterranean-style vegetable salad (see Some more ideas, page 81) and top with crumbled feta; add a baguettine and a fruit smoothie (see a home-made version on page 154)

... or brunch

Pack a wholesome snack for a combined breakfast and lunch.

• A bagel filled with low-fat soft cheese and/or tuna or pickled fish.

• Irish soda bread with smoked salmon.

• A savoury muffin (such as herb, or cheese and leek) with a tub of ricotta cheese or cottage cheese.

• A ciabatta roll filled with hard-boiled egg, lean grilled bacon or Parma ham, and sliced tomato.

Packing good things

Look at the guidelines for a healthy lunch on page 16 to help you plan imaginative and well-balanced packed lunches. Here are a few tempting ideas.

• A wedge of Spanish omelette or frittata packed with potato (see Potato and courgette tortilla, page 42), with pepper strips, cherry tomatoes and radishes.

• A baked chicken leg or thigh with home-made coleslaw and a crusty bread roll.

• Mixed bean salad topped with canned tuna, with breadsticks, ciabatta or pitta bread.

• Rice salad with smoked fish, chopped orange and mixed vegetables.

• Pasta salad with lightly cooked broccoli, sun-dried tomatoes, olives and a little cubed mozzarella cheese.

• Tabbouleh (salad of bulghur wheat, diced tomato, cucumber, fresh herbs and lemon juice) topped with poached or grilled salmon or chicken.

• Smoked mackerel dip (see Some more ideas, page 40) with vegetable and fruit crudités and oatcakes, crispbread or a wholemeal roll.

▲ From the deli, buy cured or smoked fish such as gravad lax, smoked mackerel or trout, plus bagels or rye bread and a bag of prepared salad; enjoy with some fruit juice

▲ Another great deli lunch is lean Parma ham or Spanish Serrano ham with plenty of crusty French bread, fresh fruit such as pears and figs, and a glass of red wine

• Beefsteak tomatoes filled with prawns and cottage cheese (see Some more ideas, page 85).
• New potato salad with pickled herrings, apple, cucumber and red onion.
• Falafel (see page 66), eaten cold with aubergine and apricot couscous salad (see page 84).

Instant lunches from the deli

A wide range of ready-prepared ingredients bought from a delicatessen or supermarket can make a nutritious on-the-spot packed lunch. Here are some possibilities.
• Greek or Middle Eastern mezze-style foods such as black and green olives, rice-stuffed vine leaves, dips such as hummus and taramasalata, and pitta bread.
• A selection of cheeses, with grapes, celery and oatcakes or walnut bread.
• Marinated grilled vegetables with Parmesan focaccia bread or pesto ciabatta bread.
• Goat's cheese with cherry tomatoes and olive bread.
• Cartons of fresh soup, if you have reheating facilities at work (some soups can be served cold), with crusty rolls.

A little something sweet

It's fine to include something sweet in your lunchbox if it boosts your nutritional intake. Fresh and dried fruit are obvious additions and are convenient to pack. To prevent boredom setting in, try not to get stuck in a rut with fruit – aim to buy something different every time you shop. Vary fresh fruit according to what's in season: grapes, figs, apples and pears in autumn; citrus fruits, Sharon fruit, lychees and mangoes in winter; cherries and apricots in late spring/early summer; and berries, plums and peaches in summer.

Dried fruit offers lots of possibilities, too: try ready-to-eat prunes, especially Agen or Californian prunes; mangoes, pears and peaches; apricots, particularly unsulphured apricots, which have a wonderful toffee-ish taste; ready-to-eat dried figs; raisins, especially the large, sticky Lexia raisins; and dates, such as the rich Medjool dates from Egypt and California.

There are more ideas for sweet snacks to include in your lunchbox on pages 138–150, or you could try a cereal bar (check the label to be sure it is low in fat and sugar and has a high grain and fruit content) or a small wedge of panforte (an Italian cake of pressed dried fruit and nuts).

a lighter way of eating

21

Celebration bites

We all want to indulge ourselves a little when we're celebrating or having friends over, and there's no reason why we shouldn't. Party food should be sumptuous and mouthwatering. With clever choices, it can be good for you too. Just think of smoked salmon, oysters, asparagus, luscious exotic fruits and so much more.

Special food for occasions

Whether it's a smart drinks party for friends, a celebration of a wedding, birthday or anniversary, or a festive New Year's Eve, all successful parties require a generous supply of food. Small bites that are easy to hold in the fingers are a popular way to offer food to guests, and there are lots of canapés and other morsels that can be both luxurious and nourishing. There are some tempting ideas here, for cold, hot and sweet party bites, and you'll find more on pages 110–134.

Cold finger food

• Squares of dark rye or pumpernickel bread topped with Scandinavian pickled herrings (available in jars in a variety of sauces, such as mustard, sweet, onion and tomato).
• Crostini topped with hummus, tapenade or guacamole and garnished with fresh herbs, or topped with white bean purée or tuna (see page 28).
• Cherry tomatoes stuffed with herby low-fat soft cheese or couscous.
• Pitta bread crisps (see page 30) or breadsticks with a pesto dip based on fromage frais or Greek-style yogurt.
• Mini herb scones, halved and topped with tuna, salmon or mushroom and soft cheese pâté and a garnish of sun-dried tomatoes or asparagus tips.
• Little squares of thick, flat omelette (see Potato and courgette tortilla, page 42).
• Rounds of cucumber topped with smoked mackerel dip (see Some more ideas, page 40).

• Small squares of focaccia bread topped with roasted red peppers, marinated artichokes or caramelised onions and mozzarella cheese.

Hot finger food

• Grilled spicy chicken on cocktail sticks with a satay dip.
• Tiger prawns in filo or wonton wrappers, baked (rather than fried) and served with chilli or hoisin dipping sauce.
• Blinis (small yeasted buckwheat pancakes) topped with a little soured cream and caviar, smoked salmon or gravad lax.
• Small baked new potatoes filled with a mixture of finely chopped black olives, feta cheese and fresh flat-leaf parsley.
• Angels (oysters) or devils (prunes) on horseback (wrapped in lean Parma ham and grilled).
• Grilled polenta squares topped with a thick tomato sauce and shavings of Parmesan.
• Tiny choux buns with a vegetable filling.
• Mini salmon or smoked haddock fishcakes (baked not fried).

Sweet finger food

• Little circles of brioche topped with sliced ripe peach or nectarine, sprinkled with icing sugar and grilled or baked until glazed and golden.
• Mini filo fruit tarts.
• Chocolate-dipped strawberries, cherries and pieces of pineapple (use the best-quality plain or dark chocolate).
• Little almond biscuits such as amaretti.
• A platter of ready-to-eat dried fruits, such as mango, papaya, figs, dates and apricots.
• Wedges of apple with a dip of low-fat soft cheese sweetened with maple syrup.
• Sticks of ice-cold melon – watermelon, Ogen or Galia and Charentais (perfect for a midsummer party).

Delicious cold party bites

▶ Bite-sized squares of dark rye bread topped with creamed horseradish, smoked trout and capers (front); Greek salad sticks – cubes of feta cheese, olives, cherry tomatoes and fresh basil leaves

▶▶ Mushroom and carrot sushi rolls (see Some more ideas, page 130) with wasabi paste and pickled ginger (front); thick rounds of cucumber topped with crab dip (see page 41)

Tasty hot party bites

◀◀ Mini vegetable spring rolls (see Some more ideas, page 113), front; baked new potato halves topped with guacamole (see Some more ideas, page 37)

◀ Tapenade goat's cheese toasts (see Some more ideas, page 129) made with slices of baguette (front); Scallop and prawn mini kebabs (see Some more ideas, page 110)

Tempting sweet party bites

▶ Bite-sized pieces of panettone topped with sugar-glazed banana slices (left); exotic fruit kebabs – small pieces of mango, papaya, kiwi fruit and lychee marinated in a little lime or orange juice

▶▶ Dates stuffed with low-fat soft cheese and sprinkled with cinnamon (front); wedges of pear with a dip of ricotta sweetened with honey

A dinner party

While there is no need to provide elaborate nibbles with drinks before dinner, it's nice to be able to offer your guests something when they arrive. Rather than salty crisps and roasted peanuts, serve crudités or your own pitta or vegetable crisps with a dip or salsa (see pages 30–38 for ideas), or try a healthy mix of roasted nuts (see Spiced fruits, nuts and seeds, page 44). Olives are another good nibble (you could prepare your own – see Rosemary marinated olives, page 47) as are breadsticks, oatcakes and cheese sticks (see page 134).

Afternoon tea

Afternoon tea can be delightfully dainty yet sustaining. In summer, tiny sandwiches filled with thinly sliced cucumber or fresh salmon and cakes topped with fresh fruit are traditional, while in winter toasted crumpets and teacakes are very welcome. A combination of savoury bites and wholesome cakes and biscuits, preferably home-baked, will ensure a good nutritional balance. Here are some tasty possibilities.
• Sandwiches filled with: smoked salmon; baby spinach leaves, walnuts and blue cheese; hard-boiled egg and anchovy; tuna, celery and black olive; chicken and mango chutney; prawns and rocket; turkey and cranberry relish; smoked ham, tomato and mustard; hummus and roasted pepper.
• Cheese on toast (wholemeal or Granary), cut into fingers (see Cheese and onion rarebit on page 61).
• Fruit scones spread with a little butter or low-fat soft cheese.
• Toasted crumpets, English muffins or pikelets with a savoury topping, such as yeast extract, peanut butter or cheese. Or try a sweet topping – choose from jam, marmalade or fruit compote (see Caramelised banana crumpets on page 140).
• Cinnamon toast (nicest made with Granary bread).
• Drop scones served with fresh berries and Greek-style yogurt or with maple syrup (see page 143).

For a hearty afternoon tea, serve an assortment of sandwiches and sweet delights such as drop scones, fruity teabread and biscuits, preferably home-baked

a lighter way of eating

Children love party food that is easy to hold, such as chipolatas and home-made potato crisps, pieces of fresh fruit, fruit lollipops, triangles of cheese on toast, sandwiches cut into small shapes and mini muffins

● Teabreads (see Sticky prune and ginger teabread, page 148).

● Fruit cake, made with a high proportion of fruit and nuts.

● Banana cake or carrot cake.

● Fairy cakes topped with sweetened ricotta cheese and a sliver of dried apricot or peach, or fresh berries.

● Little fresh fruit tarts made with filo pastry.

● Whisked sponge cake or roulade, filled with fresh fruit and a mixture of whipped cream and plain low-fat yogurt.

Children's parties

Children are often too excited to eat much at parties, so there's no need to overdo the preparations (unless there are adults present, who always love to dip into children's food). Many small children enjoy surprisingly strong flavours, such as garlic and curry spices. If you stick to finger food and make sure it has plenty of visual appeal, they will probably try most things – if you can get them to sit at the table for long enough! Here are some ideas, both savoury and sweet.

● Tiny sausages or chipolatas (premium high-meat-content ones), baked and then left to cool.

● Little cheese scones, halved and spread with low-fat soft cheese or fromage frais.

● Pitta bread crisps with hummus (see page 30).

● Simple sandwiches, such as grated cheese and carrot; yeast extract and ricotta; tuna or salmon and cucumber; peanut butter and diced celery (cut the sandwiches into decorative shapes with a biscuit cutter if you like).

● Little fingers or triangles of cheese on toast.

● Home-made potato crisps (see page 32).

● Spring rolls (baked rather than deep-fried).

● Fresh fruit such as small bunches of seedless grapes, whole strawberries, pitted cherries, wedges of pineapple and orange wedges (with skin for easier holding).

● Jellies made with fruit juice and containing pieces of fruit.

● Mini pavlovas filled with berries and fromage frais.

● Simple biscuits, with a guest's name iced on each one.

● Mini fruit muffins (see Summer berry muffins, page 146).

● Home-made lollipops made with fresh fruit juices or purées.

● Fruit juices diluted with mineral water.

● Fruit smoothies (see page 154).

Older children enjoy food with an element of DIY, such as pancakes or flour tortillas that they can roll up with their own choice of fillings, or baked jacket potatoes or pasta with an assortment of toppings. Another good idea is a hearty dish such as a lasagne or chilli (offer both meat and vegetarian versions) served with interesting breads and salads.

a lighter way of eating

Snacks, Nibbles and Dips

Delicious and nutritious morsels

WHEN YOU WANT A LITTLE SOMETHING to keep hunger pangs at bay, or a quick energy boost after school or exercise, a well-chosen snack is the answer. How about baked potato skins filled with creamy smoked salmon, or crisp slices of baguette topped with a garlicky white bean purée? Or dip home-made potato and beetroot crisps into a spicy peanut sauce, or tortilla chips into a zesty fruit salsa. Nibble on a crunchy mix of nuts, seeds and sweet dried fruits, or succulent marinated olives. Or try a Spanish 'tapa' – wedges of the chunky omelette called tortilla.

Tuscan bean crostini

Here's a delicious snack to be enjoyed hot or cold – toasted slices of baguette topped with a creamy white bean purée flavoured with garlic and thyme, and finished with colourful slices of tomato and leaves of rocket.

Makes 22 crostini

2 tsp extra virgin olive oil

1 small onion, finely chopped

1 garlic clove, crushed

1 can cannellini beans, about 400 g, drained and rinsed

2 tbsp crème fraîche

1 tbsp chopped fresh thyme

1 thin baguette, about 250 g (8½ oz)

3 plum tomatoes, thinly sliced

salt and pepper

rocket or sprigs of fresh herbs to garnish

Preparation and cooking time: about 25 minutes

Each crostini provides Ⓥ

kcal 62, **protein** 2 g, **fat** 2 g (of which saturated fat 1 g), **carbohydrate** 9 g (of which sugars 1 g), **fibre** 1 g

1 Heat the oil in a small frying pan, add the onion and garlic, and cook gently for about 10 minutes or until softened, stirring occasionally.

2 Meanwhile, place the cannellini beans in a bowl and mash with a potato masher or fork. Remove the pan of onion and garlic from the heat and stir in the mashed beans, crème fraîche and thyme. Season with salt and pepper to taste and mix well. Keep warm while preparing the toasts.

3 Preheat the grill to high. Cut the crusty ends off the baguette and discard, then cut the loaf into 22 equal slices, each about 1.5 cm (¾ in) thick. Toast the bread slices on both sides under the grill. (The toasts can be left to cool and then kept in an airtight tin; when ready to serve, top with the bean mixture, cooled to room temperature, and garnish.)

4 Thickly spread some bean mixture over each slice of toast, top with a tomato slice and garnish with rocket or fresh herb sprigs.

Some more ideas

• Instead of cannellini beans, use other canned pulses, such as flageolet or butter beans or chickpeas.

• Top the bean mixture with grilled courgette slices, lightly cooked button mushrooms or halved cherry tomatoes.

• Herbs such as fresh basil, oregano, sage or parsley can be used in place of the thyme.

• Use different types of bread, such as ciabatta, pugliese, wholemeal or Granary.

• Make tuna crostini. Drain and flake 1 can tuna in spring water, about 400 g. Mix with 1½ tbsp each mayonnaise and plain low-fat yogurt, 2 tbsp chopped fresh chives and pepper to taste. Spread each slice of toast with ½ tsp tomato relish or chutney, top with the tuna mixture and garnish with tiny watercress sprigs or rocket leaves.

Plus points

• Cannellini beans, popular in Italian cooking, belong to the same family as the haricot bean and have a similar floury texture when they are cooked. Though an excellent source of dietary fibre, beans can produce side effects such as bloating and wind. These can be minimised by ensuring that canned beans are thoroughly rinsed before use.

• Crème fraîche is a cream that has been allowed to mature and ferment so that it thickens slightly and develops a tangy taste. Because of its rich texture, only a little is needed to give a creamy finish.

snacks, nibbles and dips

Pitta crisps with hummus

This simple, easy-to-prepare snack is surprisingly rich in protein, vitamins and minerals. Soft pitta breads are transformed into delicious crisp fingers by brushing lightly with olive oil, sprinkling with sesame seeds and grilling. They contrast perfectly with the creamy hummus dip, made with chickpeas and fromage frais.

Serves 6

Hummus

1 can chickpeas, about 400 g, drained and rinsed

½ tsp ground cumin

2 garlic cloves, crushed

2 tbsp lemon juice

2 tbsp extra virgin olive oil

150 g (5½ oz) fromage frais

salt and pepper

paprika and ground cumin to garnish (optional)

lemon wedges to serve

Pitta crisps

6 pitta breads, about 55 g (2 oz) each

1½ tbsp extra virgin olive oil

40 g (1¼ oz) sesame seeds

Preparation and cooking time: about 15 minutes, plus cooling

Each serving provides ⓥ

kcal 319, **protein** 11 g, **fat** 14 g (of which saturated fat 3 g), **carbohydrate** 40 g (of which sugars 3 g), **fibre** 3 g

✓✓	E
✓	B₁, B₁₂, niacin, calcium, copper, iron, zinc

1 Put the chickpeas, cumin, garlic, lemon juice, olive oil and fromage frais in a food processor. Blend for 1–2 minutes or until very smooth, stopping and scraping down the sides of the container once or twice.

2 Alternatively, place the ingredients in a bowl, preferably with a flat bottom, and purée with a hand-held blender. For a slightly chunkier result, mash the chickpeas with a potato masher or fork until quite smooth, then stir in the other ingredients.

3 Season the hummus with salt and pepper to taste, then spoon into a bowl. Cover and keep in the fridge until ready to serve.

4 To prepare the pitta crisps, preheat the grill to high. Spread out the pitta breads on a baking tray and lightly brush the top side with half of the olive oil. Sprinkle with half of the sesame seeds. Grill for 1 minute or until both the bread and seeds are golden brown.

5 Turn the pittas over, brush with the remaining olive oil and sprinkle with the remaining sesame seeds. Return to the hot grill and toast for about 1 minute or until the bread and seeds are golden brown. Using scissors, quickly cut the warm pittas across into 2 cm (¾ in) fingers. Leave to cool and become crisp.

6 Sprinkle the hummus with a pinch each of paprika and cumin, if liked, then serve with the pitta crisps and lemon wedges. (The pitta crisps can be kept in an airtight tin for 1–2 days.)

Plus points

● Pitta bread, a Middle Eastern flat or unleavened bread, is a good source of starchy carbohydrate and scores low on the Glycaemic Index. It has one of the lowest fat contents of all breads.

● Chickpeas provide good amounts of dietary fibre, particularly the soluble type that can help to reduce blood cholesterol levels.

● Sesame seeds are a good source of protein, so can be particularly useful in a vegetarian diet.

snacks, nibbles and dips

Some more ideas

● For a Middle Eastern aubergine purée to serve with the pitta crisps, grill 2 medium-sized aubergines, about 450 g (1 lb) in total, turning them frequently, until soft and charred all over. Put them in a polythene bag and leave until cool enough to handle, then cut into quarters and peel them. Leave the flesh to drain in a colander for 15 minutes, then gently press to squeeze out the remaining liquid. Purée the aubergine flesh in a blender or food processor together with 1 crushed garlic clove, 1 tsp ground cumin, the juice of 1 lemon, 4 tbsp tahini paste, 1 tbsp extra virgin olive oil, 2 tbsp chopped fresh mint, and salt and pepper to taste. Garnish with a sprinkling of cayenne pepper and small fresh mint leaves, or with pomegranate seeds.

● Make Lebanese flatbread instead of pitta crisps. Split the pitta breads through the middle and carefully open them out. Put 2 tbsp toasted sesame seeds, 2 tbsp poppy seeds and 2 tbsp chopped fresh thyme in a mortar. Crush lightly with a pestle, then stir in 3 tbsp extra virgin olive oil. Spread over the inner sides of the pitta halves. Grill until golden brown, then leave to cool. Break into dipping-sized pieces to serve.

Vegetable crisps with peanut dip

Oven-baked crisps are not only healthier than those that are fried, their flavour is fresher and more concentrated too. Here, thin slices of beetroot and potato are baked in a hot oven to make dippers for a spicy South-east Asian mixture. If possible, slice the vegetables with a mandolin to ensure they are all an even thickness.

Serves 4

Spicy peanut dip

2 tsp sunflower oil

1 large shallot, finely chopped

1 garlic clove, crushed

½ tsp ground cumin

½ tsp ground coriander

55 g (2 oz) crunchy peanut butter

1 tbsp light soy sauce

1 tbsp clear honey

1 tbsp lemon juice

Vegetable crisps

2 medium-sized potatoes, about 340 g
  (12 oz) in total, scrubbed

3 medium-sized beetroot, about 340 g (12 oz)
  in total, scrubbed

2 tbsp sunflower oil

½ tsp sea salt flakes

Preparation and cooking time: about 1 hour,
  plus cooling

Each serving provides ⓥ

kcal 254, protein 7 g, fat 14 g (of which
saturated fat 2 g), carbohydrate 27 g (of
which sugars 11 g), fibre 4 g

✓✓	folate
✓	B₁, C, niacin, copper, iron, potassium, zinc

1 To make the dip, heat the oil in a small saucepan over a moderate heat, add the shallot and garlic, and fry, stirring frequently, for 3–4 minutes or until the shallot has softened and is starting to turn golden.

2 Stir in the cumin and coriander, and cook for a few more seconds, then add the peanut butter, soy sauce, honey and 4 tbsp water. Stir over a gentle heat until the ingredients are smoothly combined. Remove from the heat and mix in the lemon juice. Spoon into a small bowl, cover and set aside in a cool place while preparing the crisps.

3 Preheat the oven to 220°C (425°F, gas mark 7). Cut the potatoes and beetroot into very thin slices, about 3 mm (⅛ in), preferably using a mandolin. Alternatively, use the fine slicing blade in a food processor, or slice as thinly and evenly as possible with a sharp knife.

4 Put the potato and beetroot slices in 2 separate large bowls and add 1 tbsp sunflower oil to each bowl. Toss the vegetable slices until they are all coated lightly with oil, then spread them out, making sure they are in a single layer, on 3 large non-stick baking sheets (or on ordinary baking sheets lined with baking parchment). Sprinkle the slices evenly with the sea salt flakes.

5 Bake for 35 minutes, turning the vegetables over frequently and swapping round the position of the baking sheets each time you turn the vegetables, until the potatoes are crisp and golden and the beetroot is firm but still slightly moist. Keep a close eye on the crisps towards the end of their baking time, to be sure they do not burn, removing them as soon as they are ready. Transfer to a wire rack to cool.

6 To serve, place the bowl of dip on a large serving platter and pile the cooled crisps around it.

Plus points

• Beetroot, which was originally grown for its spinach-like leaves rather than the now more familiar dark red, swollen root, is related to the sugar beet. It has a sugar content similar to an apple. Beetroot is a good source of folate, a B vitamin essential, like the mineral iron, for healthy blood.

• Peanut butter can be made simply by grinding whole peanuts to a paste; most commercial brands add salt and sugar. Though peanut butter is high in fat, it is mostly the healthier monounsaturated type.

Some more ideas

• Parsnips and carrots also make delicious baked crisps.

• To give the vegetable crisps a spicy flavour, sprinkle them very lightly with garam masala or mild curry powder about 5 minutes before they are due to be taken out of the oven.

• For a spicy tomato dip, soften the shallot in the oil with 2 crushed garlic cloves, then stir in 1 tsp ground coriander and 1 tsp mild chilli powder. Add 200 ml (7 fl oz) passata and 1 tbsp clear honey, season with salt and pepper to taste, and simmer for 3–4 minutes or until slightly thickened. Allow to cool before serving, garnished with flat-leaf parsley.

Tortilla chips with fresh mango and tomato salsa

Here is a fresh-tasting, colourful salsa that is rich in vitamins and valuable antioxidants. It is a perfect dip for crunchy, home-made tortilla chips, quickly baked rather than deep-fried for a healthy, low-fat result. Either corn tortillas or flour tortillas can be used to make the chips.

Serves 6

8 corn tortillas, about 300 g (10½ oz) in total

Mango and tomato salsa

2 ripe mangoes, about 800 g (1¾ lb) in total

1 large ripe tomato, about 200 g (7 oz)

grated zest and juice of 1 lime

1 medium-hot fresh green chilli, seeded and finely chopped

1 garlic clove, crushed

2 tbsp chopped fresh coriander

1 tbsp snipped fresh chives

salt and pepper

Preparation and cooking time: 40 minutes, plus cooling

Each serving provides Ⓥ

kcal 214, **protein** 5 g, **fat** 1 g (of which saturated fat 0.1 g), **carbohydrate** 50 g (of which sugars 20 g), **fibre** 5 g

✓✓✓	A, C, E
✓	B₁, B₆, niacin, calcium, iron, potassium, zinc

1 Peel the mangoes and cut the flesh away from the central stone. Chop the flesh into small pieces and place in a large bowl. Chop the tomato into small pieces and add to the mango.

2 Add the lime zest and juice, chilli, garlic, coriander and chives. Stir well, then season with salt and pepper to taste. Spoon into a serving bowl, cover and set aside in a cool place while preparing the tortilla chips.

3 Preheat the oven to 160°C (325°F, gas mark 3). Cut each tortilla into wedges using kitchen scissors. Spread out the wedges on a large baking sheet and bake for 15 minutes or until crisp and firm. Transfer to a wire rack and leave to cool.

4 To serve, place the bowl of salsa on one side of a large serving platter and scatter the tortilla chips next to it.

Some more ideas

• Instead of the corn tortillas, use 4 large or 8 small flour tortillas (also called wraps), about 325 g (11 oz) in total.

• Make a fresh peach salsa by using 4 ripe peaches instead of the mangoes. There is no need to skin the peaches. Just cut them in half, remove the stone and chop them.

• For nachos, prepare the tortilla chips and leave to cool, then make a melted cheese dip. Finely chop 3 spring onions, 2 green peppers and 1 medium-hot fresh green chilli, seeded, and put into a shallow ovenproof dish. Sprinkle over ¼ tsp cumin seeds and season to taste with salt and pepper. Cut 200 g (7 oz) low-fat soft cheese into small cubes and scatter over the vegetables. Bake in a preheated 190°C (375°F, gas mark 5) oven for 10–15 minutes or until the cheese has melted. Scatter a little finely shredded Little Gem lettuce over the top, and serve hot, with the tortilla chips.

Plus points

• Fresh mangoes contain the antioxidant vitamin C, but the amount can vary considerably – in 100 g (3½ oz) mango flesh there can be as little as 10 mg vitamin C or as much as 180 mg.

• Chillies are another source of vitamin C, containing more, weight for weight, than citrus fruit such as oranges and lemons.

snacks, nibbles and dips

Baked potato skins with smoked salmon and fresh dill

Potato skins are usually deep-fried, but brushing with a mixture of olive oil and butter and then baking gives just as good a flavour and crisp texture. Here the potato skins are topped with a herby fromage frais, smoked salmon and dill filling, to make a really special and nutritious snack to enjoy with drinks.

Serves 8

8 small baking potatoes, about 200 g (7 oz) each

2 tbsp extra virgin olive oil

20 g (¾ oz) butter

125 g (4½ oz) smoked salmon

1 tbsp lemon juice

150 g (5½ oz) fromage frais

1 tbsp capers, drained and chopped

2 tbsp chopped fresh dill

salt and pepper

small sprigs of fresh dill to garnish

Preparation and cooking time: 1¾–2 hours

Each serving provides

kcal 162, protein 7 g, fat 7 g (of which saturated fat 3 g), carbohydrate 18 g (of which sugars 2 g), fibre 2.5 g

✓ B₁, B₆, B₁₂, C, folate, niacin, potassium

1 Preheat the oven to 200°C (400°F, gas mark 6). Scrub the potatoes and dry them with kitchen paper. Thread them onto metal skewers – this helps them to cook more quickly. Brush the skin of the potatoes with 1 tbsp of the oil, then sprinkle with a little salt. Arrange on a baking tray and bake for 1–1¼ hours or until tender.

2 Remove the potatoes from the skewers and cut them in half lengthways. Scoop out the flesh, leaving a layer of potato next to the skin about 1 cm (½ in) thick. (Use the scooped-out flesh for fish cakes or mash to make a savoury pie topping.) Cut each piece in half lengthways again, and place flesh side up on a large, clean baking tray.

3 Melt the butter with the remaining 1 tbsp oil and season with salt and pepper to taste. Lightly brush this mixture over the flesh side of the potato skins. Return to the oven and bake for a further 12–15 minutes or until golden and crisp.

4 Meanwhile, cut the smoked salmon into fine strips and sprinkle with the lemon juice. Mix together the fromage frais, capers and chopped dill in a bowl, and stir in the salmon.

5 Allow the potato skins to cool for 1–2 minutes, then top each with a little of the salmon and fromage frais mixture. Garnish each with a small sprig of dill, and serve while the potato skins are still warm.

Plus points

• Baking potatoes in their skins helps to retain their vitamins and minerals – many nutrients are found just beneath the skin. Eating the skins also boosts the intake of dietary fibre.

• Salmon is an oily fish and a rich source of essential omega-3 fatty acids, a type of polyunsaturated fat that is thought to help protect against heart disease. Smoking the salmon doesn't destroy the beneficial oils.

• Capers, the pickled buds of a shrub mostly grown in southern Europe, are commonly used to add a salt-sour taste, and can reduce the need for salt in a dish.

Some more ideas

● For a salmon and tomato topping, mix together 2 cans salmon, about 105 g each, well drained, 350 g (12½ oz) diced ripe tomatoes, ½ diced cucumber, 6 sliced spring onions and 12 chopped black olives. Whisk 2 tbsp extra virgin olive oil with 2 tsp red wine vinegar, 1 tsp Dijon mustard, and salt and pepper to taste. Add to the salmon mixture.

● For a chunky guacamole topping, peel and dice 2 ripe avocados, and mix with 3 tbsp lime juice, 3 tbsp Greek-style yogurt, 4 finely chopped ripe tomatoes, 1 seeded and finely chopped fresh red chilli or a dash of Tabasco sauce, and salt and pepper to taste.

● Instead of making potato skins, bake 12 small potatoes, about 125 g (4½ oz) each, for about 50 minutes or until tender. Halve the potatoes and scoop out most of the flesh, then fill with the smoked salmon and fromage frais mixture or one of the other toppings.

Spiced root vegetable wedges with creamy mustard dip

Lightly crushed coriander seeds and a hint of cinnamon accentuate the flavours of sweet potatoes, parsnips and carrots, baked in wedges to make dippers for a tangy mustard and yogurt dip. This is a terrific way to add more vegetables to your diet, to help meet the 5-a-day target.

Serves 6

2 large carrots, about 340 g (12 oz) in total

2 parsnips, about 340 g (12 oz) in total

juice of 1 lime

2 tbsp sunflower oil

2 tbsp lightly crushed coriander seeds

½ tsp ground cinnamon

600 g (1 lb 5 oz) sweet potatoes, peeled

salt and pepper

Creamy mustard dip

2 tsp wholegrain mustard

1 tsp caster sugar

grated zest of 1 lime

200 g (7 oz) plain low-fat yogurt

3 tbsp chopped fresh dill, plus extra to garnish

Preparation and cooking time: about 1¼ hours

Each serving provides ⓥ

kcal 203, **protein** 5 g, **fat** 6 g (of which saturated fat 1 g), **carbohydrate** 37 g (of which sugars 17 g), **fibre** 6.5 g

✓✓✓	A, E
✓✓	C, potassium
✓	B₁, B₆, folate, calcium, copper, iron, zinc

1 Preheat the oven to 220°C (425°F, gas mark 7). Cut the carrots across in half. Cut the narrow halves in half lengthways and each of the larger halves into quarters lengthways. Cut up the parsnips in the same way. Place the prepared vegetables in a saucepan and pour in just enough water to cover them. Bring to the boil, then reduce the heat slightly and part cover the pan. Leave the vegetables to cook for 2 minutes.

2 Meanwhile, mix together the lime juice, oil, coriander, cinnamon, and salt and pepper to taste in a large roasting tin. Cut the sweet potatoes across in half, then into thick wedges, about the same size as the pieces of carrot and parsnip. Add the sweet potato wedges to the tin and turn them in the spice mixture until they are well coated, then push them to one side of the tin.

3 Drain the carrots and parsnips and add them to the roasting tin. Use a spoon and fork to turn the hot vegetables and coat them with the spice mixture. Place the roasting tin in the oven and bake for about 40 minutes, stirring and turning the vegetables twice, until they are well browned in places and just tender.

4 While the vegetables are baking, make the dip. Mix together the mustard, sugar and lime zest, then stir in the yogurt and dill. Transfer the dip to a serving bowl, cover and set aside until the vegetables are ready.

5 Remove the vegetable wedges from the oven and leave them to cool slightly. Garnish the mustard dip with a little extra dill, and serve with the vegetables.

Plus points

• Cooking carrots increases their nutritional value – it breaks down the tough cell walls so that the body can more readily absorb the beta-carotene on offer and convert it to vitamin A. Sweet potatoes are another good source of beta-carotene.

• Parsnips were eaten by both the Greeks and Romans, but the variety common today was not developed until the Middle Ages. Being a nutritious starchy vegetable, parsnips were an important staple food before the introduction of the potato.

Some more ideas

- Coat the vegetables with a spice mixture made from lemon juice instead of lime juice, 1 tbsp caraway seeds instead of coriander seeds and ground mace instead of cinnamon. Use lemon zest instead of lime zest in the dip.
- For alternative vegetable dippers, try a mixture of 250 g (8½ oz) peeled pickling onions, 250 g (8½ oz) baby corn and 500 g (1 lb 2 oz) small new potatoes, scrubbed, instead of the carrots, parsnips and sweet potatoes. Add the whole pickling onions and baby corn to the spice mixture raw; cook the new potatoes in boiling water for 5 minutes before coating in the spice mixture. Reduce the baking time to 30 minutes.

- Make a chilli and herb dip for the vegetable wedges. Mix the plain low-fat yogurt with 1 tbsp chopped fresh mint, 2 tbsp chopped fresh coriander, 1 small fresh green chilli, seeded and finely chopped, and the grated zest of 1 lemon. Use the juice from the lemon in the spice mixture for coating the vegetables instead of the lime juice.

Piquant crab dip with crudités

This creamy dip is based on ingredients that can be kept in the storecupboard, so can be rustled up quickly if guests drop by unexpectedly. It is served with celery and cucumber sticks as well as juicy pineapple wedges, all of which add important nutrients to this snack. Breadsticks are another good dipper.

Serves 4

2 celery sticks, about 125 g (4½ oz) in total

½ cucumber, about 125 g (4½ oz)

1 small pineapple, about 340 g (12 oz)

Crab dip

1 can white crab meat, about 120 g, drained

2 tbsp mayonnaise

2 tbsp plain low-fat yogurt

1 tsp tomato purée

grated zest of 1 lime

30 g (1 oz) sun-dried tomatoes packed in oil, drained and finely chopped

30 g (1 oz) gherkins, finely chopped

a few drops of Tabasco sauce, or to taste

Preparation time: 15 minutes

1 To make the dip, put the crab meat, mayonnaise, yogurt, tomato purée, lime zest, sun-dried tomatoes and gherkins in a bowl and stir together thoroughly. Season with Tabasco sauce to taste. Place the dip in a small serving bowl, cover and chill while preparing the crudités.

2 Cut the celery and cucumber into chunky sticks. Remove the crown of leaves from the pineapple (wash and keep the leaves for garnish, if you like). Cut the flesh into wedges, leaving the skin on, then cut away the core.

3 Arrange the celery, cucumber and pineapple on a platter with the bowl of dip. Garnish with the pineapple leaves, if liked, and serve.

Some more ideas

• Use the crab dip to fill the hollows in 2 halved and stoned avocados, piling up the dip over the surface. Scatter a little diced cucumber and red pepper over the top, and serve with salad leaves and bread as a light lunch.

• Make a smoked mackerel dip. Mix 125 g (4½ oz) skinless smoked mackerel fillet with the mayonnaise and yogurt, then flavour with 1 tsp horseradish sauce, the grated zest of 1 lemon and 30 g (1 oz) chopped watercress. Garnish with sprigs of watercress. This is delicious served with medium-thick slices of crisp red and green apple as crudités.

• For canapés, serve the crab dip or smoked mackerel dip on rounds of cucumber, cut about 1 cm (½ in) thick. Garnish with thin julienne strips of radish or little watercress leaves.

Plus points

• Crab is a good source of phosphorus, a mineral needed for the development and maintenance of healthy bones. Phosphorus also plays an important role in releasing energy from food.

• Celery, first grown as a medicinal herb, only became a popular vegetable in the late 17th century. It provides potassium, and green celery sticks and leaves contain the antioxidant beta-carotene.

Each serving provides

kcal 165, **protein** 8 g, **fat** 10 g (of which saturated fat 1 g), **carbohydrate** 12 g (of which sugars 11 g), **fibre** 2 g

✓✓✓	E
✓✓	C, copper, zinc
✓	calcium, potassium

Potato and courgette tortilla

Tortilla, Spain's most famous tapa *or snack, is made from the simplest of ingredients – eggs, onions and potatoes – cooked like a flat omelette and served warm or cold, cut into wedges. All kinds of extra ingredients can be added, such as the courgette and bacon used here, or asparagus, peas and mushrooms.*

Serves 8

600 g (1 lb 5 oz) waxy potatoes, peeled and
cut into 1 cm (½ in) cubes

2 tbsp extra virgin olive oil

1 red onion, finely chopped

1 courgette, about 150 g (5½ oz), diced

2 rashers lean back bacon, derinded and
chopped

6 eggs

2 tbsp chopped parsley

pepper

Preparation time: 15 minutes, plus cooling
Cooking time: about 15 minutes

1 Add the potato cubes to a saucepan of boiling water. Bring back to the boil, then lower the heat slightly and cook for 3 minutes. Drain thoroughly.

2 Heat the oil in a heavy-based non-stick frying pan that is about 25 cm (10 in) in diameter. Add the potatoes, onion, courgette and bacon, and cook over a moderate heat for 10 minutes, turning and stirring from time to time, until the potatoes are tender and lightly golden.

3 Preheat the grill to high. In a bowl, beat the eggs with 1 tbsp cold water. Add the parsley and pepper to taste. Pour the egg mixture over the vegetables in the frying pan and cook for 3–4 minutes or until the egg has set on the base, lifting the edges to allow the uncooked egg mixture to run onto the pan.

4 When there is just a little uncooked egg on the top, place the pan under the hot grill and cook for a further 2 minutes to set the top. Slide the tortilla out onto a plate or board and allow to cool for 2–3 minutes. Cut into small wedges or other shapes and serve warm, or leave to cool completely before cutting and serving.

Some more ideas

● Instead of courgette, try chopped asparagus, or add chopped tomatoes or cooked peas just before pouring in the eggs. Fresh tarragon, chives or basil can be used in place of parsley.

● For a spicy tortilla, add ½ tsp crushed dried chillies to the beaten egg mixture.

● Make a potato, mushroom and Parmesan tortilla. Replace the onion, courgette and bacon with 200 g (7 oz) thinly sliced mushrooms and 1 sliced leek, about 200 g (7 oz). In step 2, cook the potatoes with the leek for 6 minutes, then add the mushrooms and cook for a further 4 minutes or until all the juices from the mushrooms have evaporated. Add 45 g (1½ oz) freshly grated Parmesan cheese to the beaten eggs before pouring them into the pan.

● Serve the tortilla as a light lunch for 4, with a fresh tomato salsa, leafy salad and bread.

Plus points

● Eggs provide inexpensive protein. Though they contain cholesterol, the health risks this might pose have often been over-stressed. For most people, dietary cholesterol does not raise blood cholesterol levels.

● Courgettes are a good source of vitamin B_6 and niacin. The skins contain the greatest concentration of these vitamins.

Each serving provides

kcal 165, **protein** 9 g, **fat** 8 g (of which
saturated fat 2 g), **carbohydrate** 14 g (of
which sugars 1 g), **fibre** 1 g

✓✓	B_{12}
✓	A, B_1, B_2, B_6, C, E, folate, niacin, copper, potassium, selenium, zinc

Spiced fruits, nuts and seeds

This mildly spiced mix of crunchy nuts, pumpkin and sunflower seeds, tangy dried cranberries and sweet sultanas is great for nibbling as a healthy snack or with drinks. Children love it (although it is not suitable for young children who can choke on nuts). You can easily vary the mix of nuts or fruits, depending on taste.

Makes 900 g (2 lb), to serve 16

1 tsp cardamom pods

2.5 cm (1 in) piece cinnamon stick

2 whole cloves

1 tsp black peppercorns

1 tsp cumin seeds

1 tsp coriander seeds

2 tsp finely chopped fresh root ginger

1 large egg white

25 g (scant 1 oz) fine or medium oatmeal

170 g (6 oz) blanched almonds

170 g (6 oz) pecan nut halves

170 g (6 oz) brazil nuts

85 g (3 oz) pumpkin seeds

75 g (2½ oz) sunflower seeds

115 g (4 oz) sultanas

100 g (3½ oz) dried cranberries

Preparation and cooking time: about 1¼ hours, plus cooling

Each 55 g (2 oz) serving provides Ⓥ

kcal 297, **protein** 8 g, **fat** 25 g (of which saturated fat 3 g), **carbohydrate** 10 g (of which sugars 7 g), **fibre** 3 g

✓✓✓	E, copper, selenium
✓✓	B₆, zinc
✓	B₁, niacin, iron, potassium

1 Preheat the oven to 130°C (250°F, gas mark ½). Lightly crush the cardamom pods with a pestle and mortar, or the side of a large knife, and discard the husks. Place the tiny seeds in a spice mill or a pestle and mortar, together with the cinnamon stick, cloves, peppercorns, and cumin and coriander seeds, and grind to a fairly fine powder.

2 Mix the ground spices with the ginger, egg white and oatmeal in a large bowl. Add the almonds, pecan halves, brazil nuts, pumpkin seeds and sunflower seeds, and toss well to coat them all evenly with the spice mixture.

3 Tip the nuts and seeds into a large baking tin and spread out evenly in a single layer. Bake for about 1 hour, stirring occasionally, until lightly browned and crisp. Remove from the oven and leave to cool in the baking tin.

4 Tip the nuts and seeds into a bowl. Add the sultanas and cranberries, mixing well. The mixture is ready to serve, but if not wanted immediately it can be stored in an airtight container for up to 2 weeks.

Some more ideas

● If time is short, or if you don't have a spice mill, you can use 1 tbsp ready-made curry powder or paste instead of the whole spices.

● For hot-spiced nuts and seeds, add ½ tsp crushed dried chillies and 1–2 cloves crushed garlic to the spice mixture. Use nuts and seeds only, omitting the sultanas and cranberries.

● Make sweet-spiced fruits, nuts and seeds. Replace all the spices used in the main recipe with 1 tsp ground cinnamon, ½ tsp ground ginger and ½ tsp freshly grated nutmeg. Stir these into the egg white and oatmeal, and use to coat the nuts and seeds. Bake and cool, then mix with 45 g (1½ oz) each chopped dried mango, dried cherries and chopped dried apple.

Plus points

● Almonds are rich in fat, most of it unsaturated. They are also rich in vitamin E and provide protein, fibre, and zinc and other minerals.

● Pumpkin seeds, an excellent source of beta-carotene, also contain several other antioxidants such as lutein and zeaxanthin.

● Sultanas are dried white seedless grapes. They are a rich source of natural or 'intrinsic' sugars, particularly glucose and fructose.

Rosemary marinated olives

The flavour of olives is greatly enhanced by marinating them in fruity olive oil with fresh herbs and citrus juices. When served with colourful chunks of red and yellow pepper and little cherry tomatoes, they look and taste fabulous. For the best flavour, allow about 2 days marinating. These are great with warm pitta bread fingers.

Makes 800 g (1¾ lb), to serve 8

200 g (7 oz) olives, preferably a mixture of black and green

2 tbsp extra virgin olive oil

1 tbsp lemon juice

1 thin-skinned orange, scrubbed but not peeled, cut into small chunks

2 sprigs of fresh rosemary

1 fresh green chilli, seeded and thinly sliced

1 red pepper, seeded and cut into small chunks

1 yellow pepper, seeded and cut into small chunks

125 g (4½ oz) cherry tomatoes, halved or quartered

Preparation time: 10 minutes, plus 2 days marinating

Each 100 g (3½ oz) serving provides Ⓥ
kcal 73, **protein** 1 g, **fat** 6 g (of which saturated fat 1 g), **carbohydrate** 5 g (of which sugars 4 g), **fibre** 2 g

✓✓✓	C
✓✓	A, E

1 Place the olives in a large bowl and add the olive oil, lemon juice, chunks of orange, rosemary sprigs and chilli. Stir together, then cover (or transfer to a jar and seal). Place in the refrigerator.

2 For the next 2 days, every 12 hours or so, take the olive mixture from the fridge, uncover and stir. Cover again and return to the fridge to continue marinating.

3 When ready to eat, tip the marinated olives into a serving bowl, add the peppers and tomatoes, and stir well together.

Some more ideas

• Add the marinated olives to salads, such as young spinach leaves with chickpeas, or tuna and cucumber.

• Make garlicky marinated olives with feta. Instead of orange, rosemary and chilli, add 2 roughly chopped garlic cloves, 30 g (1 oz) chopped sun-dried tomatoes and a small handful of roughly torn fresh basil leaves to the olive oil and lemon juice. Before serving the olives, toss them with 100 g (3½ oz) cubed feta cheese, the peppers, 125 g (4½ oz) halved baby plum tomatoes and some fresh basil leaves.

Plus points

• Olives are highly valued for their oil content, which is mostly the healthier monounsaturated type. Green olives provide more vitamin A than black olives.

• Extra virgin olive oil is the premium of all the olive oils. It has a low level of acidity and a wonderful aroma and flavour. As it is produced with minimal heat and refining processes, it retains more of its essential fatty acids and phytochemicals.

• The name rosemary comes from the Latin and means 'sea dew' – this strong, pungent herb was often found growing on the coast. In Roman times it was used mainly as a medicinal herb, to soothe the digestive system.

snacks, nibbles and dips

Tasty Bites on Bread

Nourishing sandwiches, both hot and cold

IT'S AMAZING WHAT YOU CAN PUT ON TOP, in between or inside bread, and how many kinds of bread there are. You could top muffin halves with Parma ham, softened leeks and mozzarella, or slices of mixed seed bread with creamy mushrooms. Split ciabatta rolls and put in grilled fresh salmon and a basil mayonnaise. Stuff pitta pockets with the chickpea patties called falafel and mixed salad, or wrap flour tortillas round smoked trout and taramasalata. Or, messy but fun to eat, fill large baps or burger buns with a sloppy minced beef and tomato mixture.

Leek and ham pizza muffins

Sweet leeks, aromatic basil and savoury Parma ham combine with mozzarella cheese to make a sophisticated pizza-style topping for wholemeal muffins. For a crisp and refreshing contrast, serve with a simple salad of watercress sprigs and coarsely grated carrot tossed with extra virgin olive oil and lemon juice.

Serves 4

1 tbsp extra virgin olive oil

2 leeks, about 250 g (8½ oz) in total, thinly sliced

4 wholemeal muffins, sliced in half

4 tbsp shredded fresh basil leaves

4 slices of Parma ham, about 50 g (1¾ oz) in total, trimmed of fat and cut in half widthways

100 g (3½ oz) mozzarella cheese, cut into thin strips

4 tbsp coarsely shredded rocket

salt and pepper

Preparation time: 15 minutes
Cooking time: 4–5 minutes

Each serving provides

kcal 310, **protein** 17 g, **fat** 14 g (of which saturated fat 4 g), **carbohydrate** 32 g (of which sugars 3 g), **fibre** 3 g

✓✓	A, E, calcium, selenium
✓	B₁, B₆, B₁₂, C, folate, niacin, copper, iron, zinc

1 Heat the oil in a saucepan, add the leeks and cook over a moderately high heat, stirring frequently, for about 5 minutes or until the leeks are tender and greatly reduced in volume. The juices they yield should have evaporated by this time – if not, increase the heat and cook for a few more seconds. Season with salt and pepper to taste.

2 Preheat the grill to high. Place the muffins, cut side down, in the grill pan without the rack. Grill to toast the bases, then turn the muffins over. Divide the leeks equally among the muffins, spreading evenly. Top with the basil, then lay a piece of Parma ham on each muffin half. Gently pinch the ham up into loose folds. Scatter the strips of mozzarella cheese over the ham.

3 Cook the muffin pizzas under the hot grill for 4–5 minutes or until the mozzarella cheese has melted and is bubbling. The ham and cheese should be lightly browned in places. Sprinkle with the shredded rocket and serve.

Some more ideas

• Use 75 g (2½ oz) lean cooked ham, cut into fine strips, instead of the Parma ham, and a handful of small watercress sprigs instead of the basil.

• For tomato and ham pizza muffins, replace the leeks with a mixture of 4 chopped ripe tomatoes, 8 chopped spring onions, 1–2 finely chopped garlic cloves and 1 tbsp chopped fresh oregano. Omit the basil. Top with the Parma ham and mozzarella cheese, and grill as in the main recipe.

• Make bacon and pineapple pizza muffins. Grill 4 lean back bacon rashers for about 5 minutes, turning once, then roughly chop or snip into pieces with scissors. Spread 4 tsp tomato purée over the split muffins and top with a mixture of 4 chopped ripe tomatoes, 3 chopped spring onions and pepper to taste. Drain a can of pineapple rings in juice, about 220 g, and cut the rings in half – there are usually 4 rings in each can. Place a piece of pineapple on each muffin half, top with the bacon and dot with 100 g (3½ oz) reduced-fat soft cheese, cut into small pieces. Cook under a hot grill for about 3 minutes or until the cheese has melted and is bubbling.

Plus points

• Leeks provide vitamin E, which has powerful antioxidant properties.

• Mozzarella contains less fat than many other cheeses, but it is still rich in calcium, essential for healthy bones and teeth and proper clotting of the blood.

Chorizo, grilled pepper and tomato bruschetta

This open sandwich of toasted ciabatta bread with a mixed pepper topping is typical of the style of food enjoyed in Mediterranean countries, where bread, along with plenty of fruit and vegetables, is a mainstay of the diet. A little chorizo sausage adds a spicy note to the sweet pepper mix.

Serves 6

1 part-baked ciabatta loaf, about 250 g (8½ oz)

1 red pepper, halved and seeded

1 yellow pepper, halved and seeded

55 g (2 oz) chorizo sausage, thinly sliced

170 g (6 oz) cherry tomatoes, quartered

2 tbsp tomato relish or chutney

15 g (½ oz) fresh basil leaves, roughly torn

1 tbsp extra virgin olive oil

1 garlic clove, crushed

black pepper

Preparation and cooking time: about 30 minutes

1 Preheat the oven to 200°C (400°F, gas mark 6). Bake the ciabatta for 8–10 minutes or according to the instructions on the packet. Remove from the oven and place on a wire rack to cool. Preheat the grill to high.

2 When the grill is hot, place the peppers skin side up on a baking tray and grill for 8–10 minutes or until the flesh softens and the skin begins to blister and char. Transfer the peppers to a polythene bag, seal with a tie and set aside until cool enough to handle.

3 While the peppers are cooling, cook the chorizo sausage in a frying pan for 3–4 minutes or until the oil runs out and the sausage slices start to crisp. Drain on kitchen paper.

4 Place the chorizo in a bowl and add the tomatoes, relish or chutney and basil. Remove the cooled peppers from the bag and peel away their skins. Roughly chop the flesh and add to the bowl. Season with pepper to taste and mix well. Set aside while you prepare the toasts.

5 Preheat the grill to high again. Cut the baked ciabatta across into 3 pieces, then cut each piece in half horizontally. Mix the olive oil with the garlic and brush this mixture onto the cut sides of the ciabatta pieces. Place them cut side up under the hot grill and toast for 2–3 minutes or until golden and crisp.

6 Top the toasted ciabatta with the pepper and chorizo mixture and serve immediately.

Each serving provides

kcal 188, **protein** 7 g, **fat** 6 g (of which saturated fat 1.5 g), **carbohydrate** 28 g (of which sugars 8 g), **fibre** 2 g

✓✓✓	C
✓✓	A, E

Plus points

- Like all breads, ciabatta is a good source of starchy carbohydrates and B vitamins. It is sometimes called 'slipper bread' because of its shape.
- Chorizo is a popular Spanish sausage made with pork and pimiento, a Spanish pepper. Though chorizo has a high fat content, this can be substantially reduced by frying the sausage in a dry pan and draining it well.

Some more ideas

• Use French bread instead of ciabatta.

• For a vegetarian topping, omit the chorizo and sprinkle the pepper and tomato mixture with 30 g (1 oz) toasted pine nuts. Or, replace the chorizo with 115 g (4 oz) crumbled feta or goat's cheese.

• Make aubergine and mozzarella bruschetta.

Slice 1 aubergine into 1 cm (½ in) thick rounds and spread them out on a baking sheet. Add 1 tsp chopped fresh thyme to 2 tbsp extra virgin olive oil and brush half of this over the aubergine slices. Place under a preheated grill and cook for about 4 minutes or until soft and lightly golden. Turn the slices over, brush with the remaining thyme oil and grill for a further

4 minutes or until lightly golden. Slice 3 plum tomatoes and 115 g (4 oz) mozzarella cheese. Overlap slices of aubergine, tomato and cheese on each toasted piece of ciabatta and grind over some black pepper. Grill for about 2 minutes, just to melt the cheese. Scatter 2–3 shredded spring onions over the top and serve immediately.

Hot and spicy tuna rolls

Here, the soft interiors of large crusty bread rolls are hollowed out to provide a crisp casing for a gently spiced mix of tuna, sweetcorn and red kidney beans, and then warmed in the oven. For a light lunch that is satisfying and well-balanced, serve with a mixed tomato and leaf salad.

Serves 4

4 large, rounded, crusty white bread rolls, about 10 cm (4 in) across, about 100 g (3½ oz) each

2 tbsp soured cream

2 tbsp mayonnaise

1 tsp hot or medium chilli sauce

2 tsp lime juice

1 can tuna in spring water, about 200 g, drained

1 can sweetcorn, about 200 g, drained

1 can red kidney beans, about 200 g, drained and rinsed

½ green pepper, seeded and diced

2 tbsp chopped fresh coriander

salt and pepper

Preparation time: 15 minutes
Cooking time: 10 minutes

Each serving provides

kcal 449, **protein** 22 g, **fat** 12.5 g (of which saturated fat 4 g), **carbohydrate** 67 g (of which sugars 8 g), **fibre** 9 g

✓✓✓	B₁₂, E, niacin, selenium
✓✓	B₁, C, copper, iron, zinc
✓	A, B₆, folate, calcium, potassium

1 Preheat the oven to 180°C (350°F, gas mark 4). Slice the tops off the bread rolls and set aside. Scoop out most of the soft interior, leaving a 'shell' about 1 cm (½ in) thick. Place the hollowed-out rolls on one side with the bread lids.

2 Make the scooped-out bread into crumbs, either by crumbling with your fingers or using a food processor. Spread 85 g (3 oz) of the breadcrumbs on a baking tray and toast in the oven for 10 minutes or until dry and crisp. Remove from the oven and set aside. Leave the oven on.

3 Mix together the soured cream, mayonnaise, chilli sauce and lime juice. Add the tuna, sweetcorn, red kidney beans, green pepper, coriander and dried breadcrumbs. Season with salt and pepper to taste. Mix together, taking care not to break up the chunks of tuna too much.

4 Spoon the tuna mixture into the hollowed-out rolls and replace the lids. Set on the baking tray and cover loosely with foil. Bake for 5 minutes, then remove the foil and bake for a further 5 minutes, to crisp the bread crust. The filling should be warm, but not bubbling. Serve immediately.

Plus points

• Using tuna canned in spring water instead of oil helps to keep the fat content of this dish low and halves the calorie content.

• Sweetcorn is a useful source of dietary fibre, which helps to keep the digestive system healthy and working efficiently. Canned sweetcorn contains carbohydrate as both starch and sugars.

• Green peppers are a good source of vitamin C. This vitamin aids the absorption of iron, particularly from non-meat sources such as the red kidney beans included in this sandwich filling.

tasty bites on bread

Some more ideas

● Make garlic mushroom rolls. Hollow out 4 sub rolls, about 115 g (4 oz) each, reserving the cut-off tops and making the scooped-out bread into crisp crumbs as in the main recipe. Slice 450 g (1 lb) button mushrooms and gently cook in a mixture of 15 g (½ oz) butter and 2 tsp extra virgin olive oil for 8–10 minutes or until tender and the juices from the mushrooms have evaporated. Add 1–2 crushed garlic cloves and

cook for a further 1–2 minutes, stirring well. Meanwhile, warm the rolls in the oven for 5 minutes. Mix the crisped breadcrumbs with the garlic mushrooms, spoon into the rolls, replace the lids and serve.

● Try scrambled egg and ham rolls. Scoop out the soft interior of the rolls and discard (or keep for another recipe). Beat 6 eggs with 3 tbsp semi-skimmed milk and salt and pepper to taste. Melt 30 g (1 oz) butter in a heavy-based

saucepan, pour in the eggs and cook over a very low heat, stirring with a wooden spoon, until the eggs start to thicken. Stir in 85 g (3 oz) cooked ham, cut into thin strips, and 2 tbsp snipped fresh chives. Continue cooking, stirring frequently, until the eggs are softly scrambled. Meanwhile, warm the hollowed-out rolls and lids in the oven or under a preheated moderate grill. Spoon the egg mixture into the rolls, replace the lids and serve immediately.

tasty bites on bread

55

Mustard fried herring roes on Granary toast

Soft herring roes, which you may also find described as herring milts, can make a dish that is both nutritious and economical. Here they are combined with fried onions, diced courgette, fresh tomato and grainy mustard, then served on thick slices of Granary bread to make a delicious lunch dish.

Serves 4

3 tbsp extra virgin olive oil

225 g (8 oz) onions, very thinly sliced

225 g (8 oz) courgettes, diced

340 g (12 oz) soft herring roes, roughly
  chopped

250 g (8½ oz) ripe tomatoes, chopped

2 tbsp wholegrain mustard

8 thick slices Granary bread, about 450 g
  (1 lb) in total

salt and pepper

watercress or rocket to garnish

Preparation time: 10 minutes

Cooking time: 15–20 minutes

Each serving provides

kcal 467, **protein** 27.5 g, **fat** 15 g (of which
saturated fat 2 g), **carbohydrate** 60 g (of
which sugars 9 g), **fibre** 7 g

✓✓✓	B₁₂, E
✓✓	B₁, C, folate, niacin, copper, iron, zinc
✓	A, B₂, B₆, calcium, potassium

1 Preheat the grill to high. Heat the oil in a large non-stick frying pan. Add the onions and cook, stirring frequently, for about 8 minutes or until they have softened and are starting to turn golden.

2 Add the courgettes to the pan and cook for a further 5 minutes, stirring frequently, until the courgettes are just tender.

3 Toss the herring roes into the pan and cook, stirring, for 2 minutes. Stir in the tomatoes and mustard, and season with salt and pepper to taste. Cook for 1 more minute or until the tomatoes have softened slightly.

4 Meanwhile, toast the slices of bread on both sides under the grill. Pile the cooked roes on top of the warm toast, garnish with watercress or rocket and serve immediately.

Another idea

● To make tomato and ginger prawns on toast, heat 2 tbsp sunflower oil in a large non-stick frying pan, add 2 tsp finely chopped fresh root ginger and 2 crushed garlic cloves, and cook for 30 seconds. Add 400 g (14 oz) chopped ripe tomatoes, 8 sliced spring onions and 2 tsp soy sauce, and cook for 5 minutes, stirring from time to time. Add 225 g (8 oz) diced courgettes and cook for a further 5 minutes to make a pulpy sauce. Stir in 225 g (8 oz) peeled raw tiger prawns and cook for 2–3 minutes or until the prawns change from blue-grey to pink. Mix in 3 tbsp chopped fresh coriander. Scatter a layer of shredded cos lettuce onto 8 toasted slices of sesame bread, then pile on the tomato and ginger prawns. Serve immediately.

Plus points

● Roes have a lot to offer in a healthy diet, being a rich source of many vitamins – A, E and the B vitamins B₁ and biotin, as well as some C and D – and low in saturated fats, so they are well worth eating more often. Herrings are full of roe just before spawning, in late summer and early autumn, and this is the best time to enjoy this dish.

● Granary bread is made from brown flour. The nutty flavour comes from the addition of malt flour and wheat kernels, which also contribute to the nutritional value. Using thick rather than thin slices is an easy way to push up the intake of starchy carbohydrates.

tasty bites on bread

Mushroom and thyme toasts

Make this whenever you are short of time and want to prepare a satisfying snack quickly. The rich flavour of chestnut mushrooms is enhanced by cooking them with garlic, herbs and a dollop of tangy crème fraîche, and they taste wonderful piled on top of toast spread with ricotta cheese.

Serves 4

125 g (4½ oz) ricotta cheese
2 celery sticks, finely chopped
3 tbsp finely chopped parsley
good pinch of cayenne pepper
500 g (1 lb 2 oz) chestnut mushrooms
1 garlic clove, crushed
2 tbsp chopped fresh thyme
2 tbsp crème fraîche
1 tsp lemon juice
8 thick slices cut from a small loaf of mixed seed bread, about 400 g (14 oz) in total
salt and pepper

Preparation and cooking time: 25 minutes

1 Put the ricotta, celery, parsley and cayenne pepper in a bowl and mix well together. Set aside in a cool place until needed. Preheat the grill to high.

2 Leave any small mushrooms whole and halve larger ones. Place them in a large, heavy frying pan, preferably non-stick, and add the garlic, thyme, crème fraîche and 1 tsp water. Cover and cook gently for 3–4 minutes or until the mushrooms are just tender and have given up their juices. Add the lemon juice and salt and pepper to taste.

3 While the mushrooms are cooking, toast the bread slices on both sides under the grill. While still warm, spread one side of each piece of toast with some of the ricotta mixture, then cut it in half.

4 Arrange the toasts on individual serving plates. Spoon the hot mushroom mixture over the toasts and serve immediately.

Another idea

• To make devilled mushroom toasts, heat 1 tbsp extra virgin olive oil in a non-stick frying pan, add 1 thinly sliced onion and cook over a moderate heat until softened. Stir in 1 crushed garlic clove, 500 g (1 lb 2 oz) halved chestnut mushrooms and 1 seeded and diced red pepper. Cook, stirring frequently, for 2 minutes, then stir in 1 tbsp Worcestershire sauce, 1 tsp Dijon mustard and 1 tsp dark muscovado sugar. Lower the heat and cook gently for 5 minutes, stirring occasionally. Add 2 tbsp chopped parsley and season with salt and pepper to taste. Toast the bread and spread with 125 g (4½ oz) soft goat's cheese. Spoon the hot devilled mushroom mixture over the toasts and serve immediately.

Each serving provides

kcal 340, **protein** 15 g, **fat** 13 g (of which saturated fat 6 g), **carbohydrate** 44 g (of which sugars 3 g), **fibre** 5 g

✓✓✓	copper, selenium
✓✓	A, B₁, niacin, calcium, iron, zinc
✓	B₂, B₆, E, folate, potassium

Plus points

• Though there are over 2,500 varieties of mushrooms grown throughout the world, not all are edible – indeed some are positively poisonous. Chestnut mushrooms tend to be larger, firmer, browner and stronger in flavour than most cultivated mushrooms. All edible mushrooms are a useful source of several B vitamins.

• Like other cheeses, ricotta is a good source of protein and calcium. Because of its high moisture content, it is lower in fat than many other varieties of soft cheese.

tasty bites on bread

58

Cheese and onion rarebit

There are many versions of Welsh rarebit (or rabbit). The one here is richly flavoured with mature Cheddar cheese and thickened with breadcrumbs to add texture, and is spooned over thinly sliced red onions before being grilled until golden and bubbling. A spinach, apple and celery salad is the perfect partner.

Serves 4

90 ml (3 fl oz) semi-skimmed milk

½ tsp mustard powder

125 g (4½ oz) well-flavoured mature Cheddar
  cheese, grated

40 g (1¼ oz) fresh wholemeal breadcrumbs

4 thick slices wholemeal bread, about 45 g
  (1½ oz) each

1 small red onion, very thinly sliced

Baby spinach, apple and celery salad

1 tbsp sunflower oil

1 tbsp walnut or hazelnut oil

2 tsp red wine vinegar

2 tsp poppy seeds

200 g (7 oz) baby spinach leaves

2 red-skinned dessert apples, quartered,
  cored and sliced

2 celery sticks, sliced

salt and pepper

Preparation time: 15 minutes, plus 5 minutes
  standing

Cooking time: 2–3 minutes

Each serving provides (V)

kcal 354, **protein** 16 g, **fat** 19 g (of which
saturated fat 8 g), **carbohydrate** 33 g (of
which sugars 10 g), **fibre** 5.5 g

✓✓✓	A, E, calcium
✓✓	folate, niacin, selenium, zinc
✓	B₁, B₂, B₆, B₁₂, C, copper, iron, potassium

---

1 Preheat the grill to high. Put the milk, mustard powder and cheese in a small heavy-based saucepan and stir over a gentle heat until the cheese has melted and the mixture is smooth. Remove from the heat and stir in the breadcrumbs. Cool for 3–4 minutes, stirring occasionally, until thickened to a spreading consistency.

2 Meanwhile, arrange the slices of bread on a baking tray and toast on both sides under the grill.

3 While the bread is toasting, make the salad. Put the sunflower oil, walnut or hazelnut oil, red wine vinegar and poppy seeds in a salad bowl, and season to taste with salt and pepper. Whisk to mix. Add the spinach, apples and celery, but do not toss.

4 Top the toast with the slices of red onion, then spoon over the cheese mixture, spreading it out to cover the toast completely. Return to the grill and cook for 2–3 minutes or until the cheese mixture is golden brown and bubbling. Toss the salad and serve with the rarebits.

Some more ideas

● For cheese and tomato rarebit, instead of the red onion use 4 firm but ripe tomatoes, thinly sliced. Add a dash of Worcestershire sauce to the cheese mixture instead of the mustard.

● Make Gorgonzola and pear rarebit. Replace the Cheddar with 55 g (2 oz) crumbled Gorgonzola cheese, and use 2 tsp wholegrain mustard instead of the mustard powder. Thinly slice 1 large, firm but ripe dessert pear and arrange on top of the toast in place of the red onion. Serve the rarebits with a crunchy side salad, made by whisking together 2 tbsp sunflower oil, 2 tbsp orange juice and salt and pepper to taste, and tossing in 1 large bunch of watercress, 85 g (3 oz) bean sprouts and 85 g (3 oz) halved red or yellow cherry tomatoes.

Plus points

● Cheddar cheese is a particularly good source of calcium, a mineral vital for the development and maintenance of healthy bones and teeth. Because Cheddar is high in saturated fat, it's a good idea to choose one that is mature and well flavoured – even a moderate amount will have a big taste impact.

● Spinach, like other dark green, leafy vegetables, is a good source of many important phytochemicals that are thought to help protect the body against several forms of cancer.

Sloppy Joes

This popular American café meal is essentially a thick bolognese-type sauce served in large toasted baps or burger buns. It is tasty comfort food that everyone, including children, will love – particularly as it is a bit messy to eat if you use fingers rather than a knife and fork – and is likely to become a firm family favourite.

Serves 4

1 medium-sized onion, chopped

340 g (12 oz) lean minced beef

1 garlic clove, crushed

1 can chopped tomatoes in rich tomato juice, about 400 g

1 tbsp tomato ketchup

1 tbsp Worcestershire sauce

1 green pepper, seeded and chopped

2 tsp chopped fresh oregano

4 large white baps, about 100 g (3½ oz) each

salt and pepper

Preparation time: 5 minutes

Cooking time: 40 minutes

Each serving provides

kcal 459, protein 30 g, fat 13 g (of which saturated fat 5 g), carbohydrate 60 g (of which sugars 10 g), fibre 3 g

✓✓✓	B₁₂, C, E, niacin, selenium, zinc
✓✓	B₁, B₆, copper, iron
✓	folate, calcium, potassium

1 Place the onion, minced beef and garlic in a large non-stick frying pan and cook over a gentle heat, stirring from time to time, for 10 minutes or until the beef is crumbly and evenly browned and the onions have softened.

2 Stir in the chopped tomatoes with their juice, the tomato ketchup, Worcestershire sauce, green pepper and oregano. Bring to the boil, then reduce the heat, cover the pan and cook gently for 30 minutes, stirring occasionally. Add a little water or stock if the mixture is beginning to look dry.

3 When the beef mixture is almost cooked, preheat the grill to moderate. Split the baps in half and toast the cut sides under the grill. Season the beef mixture with salt and pepper to taste, then pile in the baps and serve immediately.

Some more ideas

• For Tex Mex-style sloppy Joes (sloppy Josés), add 1 tsp ground cumin and a dash of chilli sauce to the minced beef mixture. Serve on thick slices of toasted sourdough bread or rolled up in soft flour tortillas.

• Instead of minced beef, try minced venison.

• Make pork and apple sloppy Joes. Use lean minced pork in place of beef and cook it with the onion and garlic as in the main recipe. In step 2, add 1 peeled and sliced cooking apple, 1 tbsp tomato chutney, 1 tsp chopped fresh sage and the grated zest of 1 orange with the canned tomatoes (omit the tomato ketchup, Worcestershire sauce, green pepper and oregano). Serve on split and toasted, crusty French baguette or ciabatta rolls.

Plus points

• Beef is much leaner than it used to be, due to changes in farming and butchering techniques – well-trimmed lean meat, including mince, can contain less than 5% fat. If you use a heavy, non-stick pan for browning mince you won't need to add any oil or butter.

• Beef offers excellent nutritional value, providing essential minerals such as iron and zinc and vitamins such as B₆ and B₁₂.

• There is no need to butter the baps, because the meat sauce is rich and juicy and moistens the bread nicely.

Grilled salmon in ciabatta

Here fresh salmon fillets are marinated, then lightly grilled and served in warm ciabatta rolls with mixed salad leaves and a basil mayonnaise, to create a very tempting and special lunch dish. Lightening the mayonnaise with yogurt reduces the fat without losing out on any of the creaminess.

Serves 4

juice of 1 lime

3 tbsp chopped fresh basil

4 pieces skinless salmon fillets, about 85 g
(3 oz) each

2½ tbsp plain low-fat yogurt

2½ tbsp mayonnaise

½ tsp finely grated lime zest

4 part-baked ciabatta rolls, about 75 g
(2½ oz) each

salt and pepper

mixed salad leaves, such as rocket, Oak Leaf
lettuce, baby spinach, red chard and lamb's
lettuce, to serve

Preparation time: 15 minutes, plus 30 minutes
marinating

Cooking time: 10 minutes

Each serving provides

kcal 408, **protein** 26 g, **fat** 18 g (of which
saturated fat 3 g), **carbohydrate** 36 g (of
which sugars 4 g), **fibre** 2 g

✓✓✓	B_{12}, E
✓✓	B_6, niacin, selenium
✓	A, B_1, folate, calcium, potassium, zinc

1 Mix together the lime juice, 2 tbsp of the basil, and salt and pepper to taste in a shallow, non-metallic dish. Add the salmon fillets and turn them in the mixture to coat well all over. Cover and leave to marinate in a cool place for 30 minutes.

2 Meanwhile, mix together the yogurt, mayonnaise, lime zest and remaining 1 tbsp basil in a small bowl. Season with salt and pepper to taste. Cover and chill until required.

3 Preheat the grill to moderate, and preheat the oven to 220°C (425°F, gas mark 7). Lift the salmon fillets out of the marinade and place in the foil-lined grill pan. Brush with a little of the marinade, then grill for 4–5 minutes on each side or until the fish is just cooked and the flesh is beginning to flake, brushing again with the marinade after you have turned the fillets. While the fish is cooking, place the ciabatta rolls in the oven to bake for about 5 minutes, or according to the packet instructions, until crisp.

4 Split the ciabatta rolls in half and spread the cut sides with the basil mayonnaise. Put a cooked salmon fillet on the bottom half of each roll and scatter over a few mixed salad leaves. Place the top half of each roll in place and serve immediately.

Some more ideas

- Use other types of rolls, such as white baps, cheese-topped rolls or seeded rolls.

- For grilled tuna baps with tomato and ginger relish, use 4 fresh tuna steaks, about 85 g (3 oz) each, and marinate them in a mixture of 2 tsp finely chopped fresh rosemary, the juice of 1 orange, and salt and pepper to taste. Meanwhile, to make the relish, sauté 1 finely chopped small red onion, 1 crushed garlic clove and 1 tbsp finely chopped fresh root ginger in 1 tbsp extra virgin olive oil for 8–10 minutes or until softened. Remove from the heat and add 4 chopped plum tomatoes, 1–2 tbsp chopped fresh basil and salt and pepper to taste. Mix well. Grill the tuna for 3 minutes on each side or until cooked to your taste, then serve in wholemeal or Granary baps with salad leaves and the relish.

Plus points

- Combining mayonnaise with low-fat yogurt not only reduces total fat, it also increases the nutritional value of the dish, in particular adding calcium, phosphorus, and vitamins B_2 and B_{12}.

- Salad leaves such as rocket are useful sources of the B vitamin folate and of beta-carotene.

Falafel pittas

Falafels, the traditional Middle Eastern bean patties, are usually deep-fried. This updated version, delicately spiced and crunchy with grated carrot, is baked for a lower fat result, but is just as delicious. When served in pitta pockets with salad and a minty yogurt dressing, the falafels make a simple, yet nutritious and filling meal.

Serves 4

1 can chickpeas, about 400 g, drained and rinsed
1 tsp extra virgin olive oil
½ tsp ground cumin
good pinch of cayenne pepper
good pinch of turmeric
1 garlic clove, crushed
1 tbsp lemon juice
1 medium-sized carrot, finely grated
1 tbsp chopped fresh coriander
4 large, oval pitta breads, about 75 g (2½ oz) each
½ cos lettuce or 1 heart of romaine lettuce, shredded
2 plum tomatoes, thinly sliced
8 tbsp plain low-fat yogurt
2 tbsp chopped fresh mint
salt and pepper

Preparation time: 15 minutes
Cooking time: 15–20 minutes

Each serving provides

kcal 379, **protein** 18 g, **fat** 5 g (of which saturated fat 1 g), **carbohydrate** 69 g (of which sugars 13 g), **fibre** 7 g

✓✓✓	A, E
✓✓	zinc
✓	B₁, B₂, B₆, C, folate, niacin, copper, iron, potassium

1 Preheat the oven to 200°C (400°F, gas mark 6). Line a baking tray with baking parchment. Put the chickpeas in a bowl with the oil and use a potato masher to mash them until quite smooth. Mix in the cumin, cayenne pepper, turmeric, garlic, lemon juice, carrot, coriander, and salt and pepper to taste. Alternatively, mix all the ingredients, except the carrot and coriander, in a food processor. Transfer the mixture to a bowl and stir in the carrot and coriander.

2 Shape the mixture into 16 flat, round patties, each about 3 cm (1¼ in) across, and place them on the parchment-lined baking tray. Bake for 15–20 minutes or until crisp and lightly browned, turning them over halfway through the cooking time.

3 About 3 minutes before the falafels have finished cooking, put the pitta breads in the oven to warm. Then split the breads in half widthwise and gently open out each half to make a pocket.

4 Half-fill the pitta bread pockets with the shredded lettuce and sliced tomatoes, then divide the falafels among them. Mix together the yogurt and mint, season with salt and pepper to taste, and drizzle over the falafels. Serve hot.

Some more ideas

- The falafels are also delicious cold, with the minted yogurt, salad and warm pitta bread.
- Make mixed bean patties with sweetcorn relish. Drain and rinse 2 cans of mixed pulses, red kidney beans or black-eyed beans, about 400 g each, then put them in a bowl and mash with a potato masher or fork. Gently fry 1 small finely chopped onion and 1 crushed garlic clove in 2 tsp extra virgin olive oil until soft. Add this to the mashed beans, together with 30 g (1 oz) fresh breadcrumbs, 1 tbsp tomato purée, a pinch of ground cinnamon, and salt and pepper to taste. Mix well, then shape into 4 patties. Brush with 1 tbsp chilli oil or extra virgin olive oil and bake as in the main recipe. Meanwhile, make the relish by mixing together 1 can sweetcorn with peppers, about 200 g, drained, 1 chopped small red onion, ½ seeded and finely chopped fresh red chilli, 1 tbsp sunflower oil, 2 tsp clear honey, 1 tbsp lime juice and 2 tbsp shredded fresh coriander. Serve the bean patties in burger buns with the sweetcorn relish.

Plus point

- Chickpeas are an important source of protein in many parts of the world. They also contain useful amounts of iron, which helps to prevent anaemia, one of the most common nutritional problems in the UK.

Egg and anchovy pan bagna

Pan bagna is a Mediterranean layered sandwich, often prepared in a hollowed-out round, rustic loaf. Here eggs, anchovies, capers, basil and tomatoes – all ingredients from a classic salade niçoise – are layered in a long French loaf, then left so that the flavours can mingle and soak into the bread. It's a great picnic lunch.

Serves 4

4 eggs

2 tbsp extra virgin olive oil

1 garlic clove, crushed

1 large French baguette, about 25 cm (10 in) long, about 225 g (8 oz)

3 ripe tomatoes, sliced

1 red or yellow pepper, seeded and very thinly sliced

½ mild Spanish onion, very thinly sliced

8 anchovy fillets, halved lengthways

1 tbsp drained capers

a good handful of fresh basil leaves

pepper

Preparation and cooking time: 25 minutes, plus 1 hour soaking

Each serving provides

kcal 347, **protein** 17 g, **fat** 16 g (of which saturated fat 3 g), **carbohydrate** 38 g (of which sugars 7 g), **fibre** 2 g

✓✓✓ A, B₁₂, C, E

✓✓ niacin, selenium

✓ B₁, B₂, B₆, folate, calcium, copper, iron, potassium, zinc

1 Place the eggs in a pan with enough cold water to cover them. Bring to the boil, then lower the heat slightly so that the water is boiling gently, and cook the eggs for 8 minutes. Drain and rinse the eggs under cold running water to cool them quickly. Peel and slice.

2 Stir the oil and garlic together in a small bowl. Cut the bread open lengthways, keeping it still attached along one side, like a hinge. With the loaf opened out flat, drizzle the garlic-flavoured oil all over the cut sides.

3 Layer the egg slices, tomatoes, pepper, onion and anchovies in the baguette, scattering on the capers and basil leaves among the layers. Make sure that each ingredient is evenly distributed along the loaf. Season with pepper, then close up the loaf and wrap in cling film.

4 Leave at cool room temperature for about 1 hour (or up to 3 hours in the fridge). Slice across into 4 portions for serving.

Some more ideas

• For a more substantial sandwich, add 85 g (3 oz) drained canned tuna or pan-seared fresh tuna steak, flaked.

• Instead of red or yellow pepper, try roasted peppers or marinated artichoke hearts.

• Make a Greek-style salad loaf. Layer 200 g (7 oz) sliced halloumi cheese, 1 sliced red onion, 3 sliced ripe tomatoes, 100 g (3½ oz) thinly sliced cucumber, 55 g (2 oz) stoned black olives and a small handful of fresh mint leaves in the baguette.

Plus points

• Anchovies are small oily fish, most commonly available filleted and cured by salt or brine. They contain both calcium and phosphorus, essential for healthy bones and teeth. These minerals are still present in anchovies that have been cured and canned or bottled.

• The powers of garlic have been recognised for centuries and it has been credited with curing complaints as diverse as athlete's foot and the common cold. The discovery of allicin, the compound that gives garlic its characteristic smell and taste, and its anti-fungal and antibiotic properties, supports already established folklore.

Sardine, watercress and carrot open sandwich

This unusual combination of ingredients makes a colourful sandwich that is packed with interesting textures and good flavours. It only takes a few minutes to make, so is perfect for a quick lunch or a snack at any time.

Serves 4

1 carrot, about 125 g (4½ oz), grated

30 g (1 oz) watercress, roughly chopped

2 tbsp chopped fresh chives

150 g (5½ oz) reduced-fat soft cheese

8 thick slices rye bread

2 cans sardines in olive oil, about 120 g each, drained

1 small red onion, thinly sliced

pepper

a few long fresh chives to garnish

Preparation time: 10 minutes

1 Mix the grated carrot, watercress and chives into the soft cheese. Season to taste with pepper.

2 Spread the cheese mixture evenly over one side of each slice of rye bread. Halve the sardines lengthways, then arrange them, skin side up, on top of the cheese.

3 Arrange the red onion slices over the sardines and top with a few long pieces of chive to garnish. Sprinkle with pepper and serve.

Some more ideas

• For a different texture and flavour, try multigrain bread instead of rye bread.

• To reduce the fat content, use sardines canned in brine rather than in oil, and fromage frais instead of reduced-fat soft cheese.

• For a packed lunch or picnic, make hearty 'closed' sandwiches, with 2 slices of bread for each one.

• Try smoked mackerel and apple open sandwiches. Mix the soft cheese with 1 grated crisp dessert apple, 2 tbsp finely chopped cucumber and the chives. Spread over multigrain or rye bread and top with 175 g (6½ oz) flaked smoked mackerel fillet. Garnish with thin slices of radish.

Plus points

• In the Middle Ages, the early varieties of carrot were red, purple or black in colour due to the presence of anthocyanin pigments. It was not until the 17th century that the now familiar orange carrot was introduced. Its orange colour is due to beta-carotene. The beta-carotene content can vary according to variety and age, with more of this antioxidant usually found in older, dark orange carrots and less in young, pale orange ones.

• Sardines are really young pilchards, although the young of other fish such as sprats and herrings may also be called sardines. They are rich in omega-3 fatty acids and contain the type of iron easily absorbed by the body. In addition, eating the bones of canned fish such as sardines will boost calcium intake.

• Mixing grated carrot and chopped watercress into a soft cheese sandwich filling is a good way to encourage children to eat more vegetables.

Each serving provides

kcal 331, **protein** 20 g, **fat** 14 g (of which saturated fat 6 g), **carbohydrate** 33 g (of which sugars 6 g), **fibre** 4 g

✓✓✓	A, B₁₂
✓✓	E, niacin, calcium, selenium, zinc
✓	B₁, B₂, B₆, C, folate, copper, iron, potassium

tasty bites on bread

Smoked trout wraps

Wraps are made by rolling up a filling inside a soft, wheat flour tortilla. They make a great alternative to ordinary sandwiches. Here smoked trout, taramasalata and salad greens combine for a tempting filling.

Serves 8

8 large flour tortillas, about 340 g (12 oz) in total

170 g (6 oz) taramasalata

85 g (3 oz) watercress

½ cucumber, thinly sliced

4 skinless smoked trout fillets, about 75 g (2½ oz) each, flaked

Preparation and cooking time: 15 minutes

1 Preheat the oven to 180°C (350°F, gas mark 4). Wrap the stack of tortillas in foil and warm in the oven for 10 minutes or according to the packet instructions.

2 Spread a little taramasalata on the centre of each warm tortilla, then scatter over the watercress, cucumber slices and smoked trout pieces. Roll up tightly to enclose the filling. Cut each rolled tortilla in half diagonally and serve immediately.

Some more ideas

• Instead of regular taramasalata, you can use reduced-fat taramasalata, which is widely available in supermarkets.

• Make hoisin chicken wraps, a twist on the popular Chinese crispy duck with pancakes. Cut 250 g (8½ oz) cooked, skinless boneless chicken breasts (fillets) into thin slices. Cut ½ cucumber into thin sticks and shred 6 spring onions. Spread each warm tortilla with 2 tsp hoisin sauce, then place some chicken, cucumber and spring onion on top and roll up the tortillas tightly. Cut each in half to serve. Smoked chicken breast or skinned, roasted duck breast can also be used.

Plus points

• Tortillas are very thin, pancake-like breads, which may be made from a wheat flour dough or a special maize meal called *masa harina*. A staple in the Central American diet, tortillas provide an alternative to the more commonly eaten breads and are another way to include starchy carbohydrates in the diet. Wrapped around a filling, they are easy and fun to eat.

• Trout is an oily fish with a high content of the essential omega-3 fatty acids. These can help to protect the body against strokes and heart disease. Trout also contains high levels of vitamin E, which helps to protect cells from damage by free radicals.

• Cucumber, the fruit of a climbing member of the gourd family, has a very high water content (96%), which means it is very low in calories. The skin contains beta-carotene.

Each serving provides

kcal 275, **protein** 12 g, **fat** 14 g (of which saturated fat 1 g), **carbohydrate** 27 g (of which sugars 1 g), **fibre** 1 g

✓✓✓ B$_{12}$

✓ A, B$_1$, C, E, niacin, calcium, selenium

Lunches for All Occasions

Good ways to recharge batteries

IN THE MIDDLE OF THE DAY, IT'S ESSENTIAL to have a bite to eat, to boost flagging energy levels. When you feel like something more substantial than a sandwich, why not try a salad of chicken tossed with spinach and oranges in a tarragon dressing? A fresh salmon chowder might appeal, or an easy 'hash' of smoked haddock, potato and cabbage. You could also make an omelette or a light cheesy soufflé, or a dish of pasta baked with aubergine. Stuffed pancakes, a meal-in-a-bowl risotto and couscous-filled tomatoes are other tempting possibilities.

Fennel and bean salad

The pleasant aniseed flavour of fresh fennel combines with flageolet beans, green olives, Parma ham and a fresh orange dressing in this appetising warm salad. Serve it with crusty French bread for a satisfying lunch.

Serves 4

grated zest and juice of 1 small orange

1 tsp wholegrain mustard

1½ tbsp extra virgin olive oil

1 garlic clove, crushed

1 can flageolet beans, about 400 g, drained and rinsed

75 g (2½ oz) stoned green olives

1 large bulb of fennel, about 340 g (12 oz), sliced

150 g (5½ oz) green beans, halved

2 courgettes, about 250 g (8½ oz) in total, sliced

6 slices Parma ham, about 85 g (3 oz) in total, fat removed and slices halved

salt and pepper

Preparation and cooking time: 20–25 minutes

Each serving provides

kcal 221, **protein** 14 g, **fat** 10 g (of which saturated fat 2 g), **carbohydrate** 19 g (of which sugars 7 g), **fibre** 9 g

✓✓	C, E, folate, potassium
✓	A, B₁, B₆, calcium, zinc

1 Mix together the orange zest and juice, mustard, olive oil and garlic in a gratin or other shallow baking dish. Add the flageolet beans and olives and toss well. Season with salt and pepper to taste, then set aside while preparing the rest of the salad.

2 Bring a pan of salted water to the boil, add the fennel and green beans, and simmer for 1 minute. Add the courgettes and cook for a further 3–4 minutes or until the vegetables are just tender. Meanwhile, preheat the grill to high.

3 Drain the vegetables and toss them with the flageolet beans and olives in the gratin dish. Scrunch up the pieces of Parma ham and arrange on top. Place the dish under the grill and cook for 1–2 minutes, just to warm the ham, then serve immediately.

Another idea

● To make a pepper and cannellini bean salad with omelette strips, combine 1 crushed garlic clove, 1 finely chopped shallot, 2 tbsp extra virgin olive oil, 1 tsp balsamic vinegar, 2 tbsp shredded fresh basil, and salt and pepper to taste in a salad bowl. Whisk to mix. Add 2 red peppers, seeded and roughly chopped, 1 can cannellini beans, about 410 g, drained and rinsed, and 75 g (2½ oz) stoned black olives. Cook 115 g (4 oz) green beans in boiling water for 4 minutes, then drain and refresh under cold running water. Add to the bowl. Beat together 3 large eggs and 3 tbsp water, then stir in 2 tbsp shredded fresh basil and 2 tbsp snipped fresh chives. Heat 1 tbsp extra virgin olive oil in a 20 cm (8 in) non-stick frying pan, pour in the egg mixture and cook for 2–3 minutes or until the omelette is set, lifting the edges so the liquid egg can run onto the pan. Cut the omelette into strips, place on top of the salad and serve.

Plus points

● Bulb fennel was first cultivated by the Egyptians. It provides useful amounts of potassium and folate, as well as phytoestrogen, a naturally occurring plant hormone that may be helpful in protecting against breast cancer.

● Parma ham is the best known of the Italian salted, air-dried prosciuttos (the Italian word for ham). It is very lean, as long as you trim off visible fat, and has a wonderful flavour.

Sugarsnap salad with black grapes and feta cheese

Sugarsnap peas, with their full flavour and crisp texture, work well with baby spinach leaves and a little peppery rocket to provide the salad base for tangy feta cheese and sweet black grapes. Serve this quickly prepared lunch dish with thick slices of warm country-style bread or pitta bread.

Serves 4

grated zest and juice of ½ lemon
½ tsp caster sugar
½ tsp Dijon mustard
1 tbsp extra virgin olive oil
300 g (10½ oz) sugarsnap peas
200 g (7 oz) seedless black grapes, halved
200 g (7 oz) feta cheese, cut into thin strips
45 g (1½ oz) rocket, shredded
170 g (6 oz) baby spinach leaves
salt and pepper

Preparation time: about 20 minutes

Each serving provides Ⓥ

kcal 221, **protein** 12 g, **fat** 14 g (of which saturated fat 7 g), **carbohydrate** 14 g (of which sugars 13 g), **fibre** 3 g

✓✓✓	A, C
✓✓	B₁₂, E, folate, calcium
✓	B₁, B₂, B₆, niacin, copper, iron, potassium, zinc

1 Place the lemon zest and juice in a large salad bowl. Add the sugar and mustard with salt and pepper to taste. Whisk the ingredients together until the sugar and salt have dissolved in the lemon juice. Whisk in the olive oil.

2 Cut the sugarsnap peas across in half. Bring a large pan of water to the boil, add the sugarsnap peas and bring back to the boil. Immediately drain the sugarsnaps and refresh under cold running water. Add them to the salad bowl, and turn and fold to coat them with the dressing.

3 Add the grapes, feta cheese, rocket and spinach to the bowl, and mix the salad gently but well, so that all the ingredients are coated with dressing. Serve at once.

Some more ideas

• Instead of rocket, add 6 chopped spring onions.
• For a garlicky dressing, add 1 finely chopped garlic clove with the sugar and mustard.
• Add extra crunch by sprinkling the salad with 2 tbsp toasted pine nuts just before serving.
• Make a pear, grape and spinach salad with blue cheese dressing. For the dressing, crumble or chop 50 g (1¾ oz) Danish blue cheese and place it in the salad bowl, then stir in 1 tbsp cider vinegar and 2 tbsp extra virgin olive oil. Halve and core 2 ripe but firm dessert pears, then cut them across into slices. Add the pear slices to the blue cheese dressing as they are prepared. Add the halved black grapes and mix well, then add 45 g (1½ oz) watercress, 200 g (7 oz) baby spinach leaves and 2 tbsp chopped walnuts. Toss together gently and serve immediately.

Plus points

• Sugarsnap peas, like mange-tout, are eaten pods and all. They have a deliciously sweet taste and tender texture, and are a good source of dietary fibre and vitamin C.
• Feta cheese is high in fat and salt, but because its flavour is strong a little can go a long way in a salad. As with other cheeses, it is a good source of protein, calcium and phosphorus, and provides useful amounts of B vitamins and vitamin E.
• Black grapes contain bioflavonoids, natural plant chemicals that act as antioxidants and help to protect against damage caused by free radicals.

Middle Eastern salad

Based on fattoush, *the colourful, crunchy salad served throughout the Middle East, this version adds tuna fish for extra flavour and protein. Make sure you grill the pitta bread until really crisp to prevent it from going soggy when mixed with the other ingredients, and serve the salad as soon as possible after making.*

Serves 4

4 pitta breads, about 55 g (2 oz) each

3 tbsp extra virgin olive oil

juice of 1 lemon

6 spring onions, sliced

340 g (12 oz) ripe tomatoes, chopped

½ cucumber, diced

1 can tuna in spring water, about 200 g, drained and flaked

2 tbsp coarsely chopped fresh flat-leaf parsley

1 tbsp coarsely chopped fresh coriander

1 tbsp coarsely chopped fresh mint

salt and pepper

Preparation time: about 15 minutes

Each serving provides

kcal 311, **protein** 18 g, **fat** 11 g (of which saturated fat 2 g), **carbohydrate** 36 g (of which sugars 5 g), **fibre** 3 g

✓✓✓	B₁₂, C, E, selenium
✓✓	niacin
✓	A, B₁, B₆, folate, calcium, copper, iron, potassium, zinc

1 Preheat the grill to high. Warm the pitta breads under the grill for a few seconds or until puffy, then carefully split them open through the middle and open out each one like a book. Return to the grill and toast for 2–3 minutes on each side or until lightly browned and crisp. Roughly tear the pitta into bite-sized pieces and set aside.

2 Whisk together the olive oil and lemon juice in a large serving bowl, and season with salt and pepper to taste. Add the spring onions, tomatoes, cucumber and tuna, and toss gently to coat with the oil and lemon juice.

3 Add the parsley, coriander, mint and torn pitta pieces to the serving bowl and toss quickly to mix. Serve immediately.

Some more ideas

• Make a more substantial salad by adding 1 can black-eyed or aduki beans, about 400 g, drained and rinsed.

• For a Mediterranean-style vegetable salad, whisk together 1 tsp Dijon mustard, 1 tsp finely grated lemon zest, 1 crushed garlic clove, 2 tsp red wine vinegar, 2 tbsp extra virgin olive oil, 1 tbsp chopped fresh oregano, and salt and pepper to taste in a large serving bowl. Quarter 250 g (8½ oz) baby plum tomatoes and add to the bowl. Add 2 medium-sized courgettes, 1 small bulb of fennel and 1 red onion, all coarsely chopped. Toss to coat the vegetables with the dressing. Serve this salad with sardine toasts for extra protein and carbohydrate. Drain 1 can sardines in olive oil, about 120 g, and roughly mash with 2 tsp drained capers. Cut 12 slices of ciabatta or French bread, each about 1 cm (½ in) thick, and toast on both sides. Spread the mashed sardines on one side of each slice. Sprinkle with 2 tbsp freshly grated Parmesan cheese and grill for about 1 minute or until golden brown.

Plus points

• Tomatoes, like so many other fruits and vegetables, are a good source of the antioxidants beta-carotene and vitamin C. They also contain lycopene, a carotenoid compound that acts as an antioxidant and which is thought to be very important in helping to prevent the development of cancer.

• Using both the white bulb and leaves of spring onions increases the beta-carotene provided, as this all-important antioxidant is found in the green part of the vegetable.

Tarragon chicken salad

Tahini, a paste made from ground sesame seeds, is a favourite ingredient in Middle Eastern cooking. Available from most large supermarkets, it adds a nutty taste and thick creaminess to the dressing for this colourful and nutritious chicken salad. Serve with warmed crusty rolls.

Serves 4

2 skinless boneless chicken breasts (fillets), about 300 g (10½ oz) in total

360 ml (12 fl oz) chicken or vegetable stock

1 small bunch of fresh tarragon

1 small lemon

3 black peppercorns

2 tbsp tahini

1 head chicory, about 150 g (5½ oz)

140 g (5 oz) baby spinach leaves

2 oranges

45 g (1½ oz) flaked almonds, toasted

salt and pepper

Preparation and cooking time: 40 minutes

Each serving provides

kcal 345, **protein** 27 g, **fat** 23 g (of which saturated fat 3 g), **carbohydrate** 10 g (of which sugars 8 g), **fibre** 5 g

✓✓✓ C, E, niacin, copper, potassium

✓✓ A, B$_1$, B$_6$, folate, calcium, iron, zinc

✓ B$_2$, selenium

1 Put the chicken breasts in a shallow pan, in one layer, and pour over the stock. Remove the tarragon leaves from the stalks and set them aside. Lightly crush the tarragon stalks with a rolling pin to release all their flavoursome oils, then add to the pan. Using a vegetable peeler, remove a small strip of zest from the lemon and add this to the pan together with the peppercorns.

2 Set the pan over a moderate heat and bring the stock to the boil. Turn down the heat so the stock just simmers gently and cover the pan. Cook for 15 minutes or until the chicken is white all the way through.

3 Remove the chicken breasts using a draining spoon and leave to cool on a plate. Strain the stock into a jug and discard the tarragon stalks, lemon zest and peppercorns. Set the stock aside. When the chicken has cooled, cut it into thick strips.

4 Put the tahini into a mixing bowl and gradually whisk in 4 tbsp of the reserved stock to make a smooth, creamy dressing. If the dressing is a bit thick, whisk in another 1–2 tbsp of the stock. Squeeze the juice from the lemon and stir it into the dressing. Chop enough of the tarragon leaves to make 1 tbsp, and add to the dressing with salt and pepper to taste.

5 Cut the chicory across on the diagonal into slices about 1 cm (½ in) thick. Arrange the chicory and spinach in a large salad bowl.

6 Peel the oranges, then cut between the membrane into segments. Scatter the segments over the salad leaves, followed by the toasted almonds. Place the chicken strips on top, and spoon over the tahini tarragon dressing. Serve immediately.

Plus points

• Chicken is an excellent source of protein and provides many B vitamins. Removing the skin reduces the fat content considerably, as most of the fat in chicken lies directly beneath the skin.

• Chicory was used by the ancient Egyptians, Greeks and Romans, both for its medicinal properties and for cooking. It was believed to stimulate the digestive juices and strengthen the liver.

lunches for all occasions

Another idea

● For an Oriental chicken salad, poach the chicken in stock flavoured with 3 thin slices fresh root ginger and 3 black peppercorns. Combine 150 g (5½ oz) shredded Chinese leaves, 100 g (3½ oz) cos lettuce, torn into pieces, and 50 g (1¾ oz) watercress in a large salad bowl, and arrange the sliced chicken on top. Scatter over 3 peeled and diced kiwi fruit. For the dressing, whisk together 2 tbsp tahini, 1 crushed garlic clove, 1 tsp finely chopped fresh root ginger, the grated zest and juice of 1 lemon, 1 tbsp light soy sauce, a good pinch of five-spice powder and 3–4 tbsp of the reserved poaching stock until smooth and with a light coating consistency. Spoon the dressing over the salad, sprinkle with 2 tbsp sesame seeds and serve with warm pitta breads.

Spiced couscous tomatoes

Choose ripe, well-flavoured tomatoes for this dish. Hollowed out, they make the perfect container for a spicy aubergine, dried apricot and nut couscous. The vitamin C-rich juices are squeezed out of the scooped-out tomato flesh and seeds, and whisked with a little harissa paste to make a tangy dressing. Serve with sesame breadsticks.

Serves 4

8 large beefsteak tomatoes, about 170 g (6 oz) each

1½ tbsp extra virgin olive oil

55 g (2 oz) flaked almonds

1 small aubergine, about 170 g (6 oz), cut into 1 cm (½ in) dice

1 tsp ground coriander

½ tsp ground cumin

pinch of ground cinnamon

240 ml (8 fl oz) boiling vegetable stock

125 g (4½ oz) couscous

2 tbsp chopped fresh mint

55 g (2 oz) ready-to-eat dried apricots, chopped

1 tsp harissa paste

salt and pepper

Preparation and cooking time: 25 minutes

Each serving provides ⓥ

kcal 326, **protein** 11 g, **fat** 14 g (of which saturated fat 2 g), **carbohydrate** 40 g (of which sugars 18 g), **fibre** 6 g

✓✓✓	A, C, E
✓✓	potassium
✓	B₁, B₆, folate, niacin, calcium, copper, iron, zinc

---

1 Cut the tops off the tomatoes and scoop out the insides using a teaspoon. Place the hollowed-out tomatoes and cut-off tops on one side. Put the seeds and scooped-out flesh in a sieve set over a small jug or bowl and press with the back of a spoon to extract the juices; you will need about 4 tbsp. Leave the jug of juice on one side and discard the seeds and flesh.

2 Sprinkle a little salt over the insides of the hollowed-out tomatoes. Place them upside-down on a plate covered with kitchen paper and leave to drain while making the filling.

3 Heat ½ tbsp of the olive oil in a non-stick saucepan. Add the flaked almonds and cook over a low heat for 2–3 minutes or until golden brown. Remove from the pan with a draining spoon and set aside.

4 Add the remaining 1 tbsp oil to the saucepan. Stir in the aubergine and cook for 5 minutes, turning frequently, until browned and tender. Stir in the coriander, cumin and cinnamon, and cook for a few more seconds, stirring constantly.

5 Pour in the stock and bring to a rapid boil, then add the couscous in a steady stream, stirring constantly. Remove from the heat, cover and leave to stand for 5 minutes.

6 Uncover the pan, return to a low heat and cook for 2–3 minutes, stirring with a fork to separate the couscous grains and fluff them up. Stir in the toasted almonds, mint and dried apricots.

7 Add the harissa paste to the reserved tomato juices and stir to mix, then pour over the couscous. Season with pepper to taste and mix well. Spoon the couscous mixture into the tomatoes, replace the tops and serve.

Plus points

● The presence of vitamin C in a dish – here provided by the tomatoes – improves the body's absorption of iron from grain products such as couscous and from dried apricots.

● Couscous is low in fat and high in starchy carbohydrates and fibre. It has a moderate score on the Glycaemic Index, which means that it is digested and absorbed relatively slowly, releasing glucose gradually into the blood stream. This helps to keep blood sugar levels steady.

lunches for all occasions

Some more ideas

• Use courgettes instead of aubergine.

• Dried peaches and hazelnuts or pine nuts can be used in place of dried apricots and almonds.

• For tomatoes filled with prawns and cottage cheese, whisk together 1 tbsp sunflower oil, 1 tsp lemon juice, 2 tbsp chopped fresh dill and 2 finely chopped gherkins with salt and pepper to taste. Stir in ½ finely diced cucumber and 2 grated carrots. Leave this to marinate while preparing the tomatoes as in the main recipe. Stir 250 g (8½ oz) cottage cheese and 170 g (6 oz) cooked peeled prawns into the cucumber and carrot mixture, then spoon into the hollowed-out tomatoes and replace the tops.

Salmon and tomato chowder

A chowder is a classic American meal-in-a-bowl soup. The name is derived from the French word chaudière, *meaning 'stew-pot'. This delicious chowder is flavoured with lean bacon, leeks and tomatoes and thickened with potatoes, all of which provide the perfect background for tender flakes of salmon. Try it with sourdough bread.*

Serves 4

200 g (7 oz) piece of skinless salmon fillet
1 bay leaf
300 ml (10 fl oz) fish or vegetable stock
600 ml (1 pint) semi-skimmed milk
15 g (½ oz) unsalted butter
1 tsp sunflower oil
1 large onion, finely chopped
1 leek, chopped
1 thick rasher back bacon, about 30 g (1 oz),
    derinded and chopped
340 g (12 oz) potatoes, peeled and diced
340 g (12 oz) tomatoes, skinned, seeded and
    diced
3 tbsp chopped parsley
4 tbsp Greek-style yogurt
salt and pepper

Preparation time: 15 minutes
Cooking time: 30 minutes

Each serving provides

kcal 358, **protein** 22 g, **fat** 16 g (of which saturated fat 7 g), **carbohydrate** 33 g (of which sugars 17 g), **fibre** 4 g

✓✓✓	B_6, B_{12}, C, E
✓✓	A, B_1, B_2, folate, niacin, calcium, potassium, selenium, zinc
✓	copper, iron

1 Put the salmon in a large saucepan with the bay leaf. Pour over the stock and add some of the milk, if needed, so the fish is covered with liquid. Slowly bring to the boil, then cover the pan and simmer over a low heat for 6–7 minutes or until the fish will flake easily. Remove the salmon with a draining spoon and break into large flakes, discarding any bones. Set aside. Pour the cooking liquid (with the bay leaf) into a jug or bowl and reserve.

2 Heat the butter and oil in the saucepan. Add the onion, leek and bacon, and cook over a low heat for 10 minutes or until soft, stirring frequently. Add the potatoes and cook for a further 2 minutes, stirring constantly.

3 Pour over the reserved cooking liquid and add the remaining milk. Bring to the boil, then half-cover the pan with a lid and simmer for 8 minutes, stirring occasionally. Add the tomatoes and cook for a further 3–4 minutes or until the potatoes are just tender, but have not started to disintegrate.

4 To thicken the soup, remove a ladleful or two and purée it in a bowl with a hand-held blender, or in a food processor, then return it to the soup in the pan and mix well.

5 Stir in the flaked salmon and 2 tbsp of the parsley. Simmer gently for 1–2 minutes or until the soup is piping hot. Discard the bay leaf. Season with salt and pepper to taste.

6 Ladle the soup into warmed serving bowls. Top each serving with 1 tbsp yogurt, swirling it round, and add a sprinkling of the remaining chopped parsley. Serve hot.

Plus points

● Salmon is an excellent source of protein as well as of vitamins B_6 and B_{12} and the minerals selenium and potassium. It also offers heart-healthy fats.

● Milk provides several important nutrients, most notably protein, calcium, phosphorus and many of the B vitamins. These nutrients are found in the non-fat part of milk, so lower fat varieties, such as semi-skimmed milk, actually contain more than full-fat milk.

Some more ideas

● For a sweetcorn and blue cheese chowder, soften 1 chopped onion and 1 chopped celery stick in 15 g (½ oz) butter. Stir in 340 g (12 oz) peeled and diced potatoes, 450 ml (15 fl oz) semi-skimmed milk, 300 ml (10 fl oz) vegetable stock and 1 bay leaf. Half-cover and simmer for 12 minutes or until the potatoes are tender. Purée one-third of the soup in a food processor or with a hand-held blender, then mix it with the rest of the soup. Stir in 1 can cream-style sweetcorn, about 420 g, 3 tbsp snipped fresh chives and salt and pepper to taste. Simmer for 2–3 minutes to heat through. Ladle into serving bowls and top each one with 1 tbsp fromage frais and 30 g (1 oz) crumbled blue cheese.

● Make a quick and easy clam chowder. Soften 1 bunch sliced spring onions in 15 g (½ oz) butter. Add 340 g (12 oz) peeled and diced potatoes, 450 ml (15 fl oz) fish stock and 300 ml (10 fl oz) semi-skimmed milk. Half-cover and simmer for 12 minutes or until the potatoes are tender. Mash a few of the potatoes on the side of the pan to thicken the soup, then stir in 2 cans clams, about 175 g each, well drained, 1 can cream-style sweetcorn, about 420 g, 1 can chopped tomatoes, about 200 g, with the juice, 3 tbsp chopped parsley, 2 tbsp dry sherry and salt and pepper to taste. Simmer for about 5 minutes or until piping hot.

Japanese soup noodles with smoked tofu and bean sprouts

As interest in Oriental cuisines increases, supermarkets are stocking a wider variety of noodles. To make this tempting lunch dish, Japanese soba – hearty noodles made from buckwheat – are simmered in a soy and ginger stock with smoked tofu and an appetising mixture of vegetables.

Serves 4

150 g (5½ oz) soba (Japanese buckwheat noodles)

1 tbsp sunflower oil

1 tbsp finely grated fresh root ginger

2 garlic cloves, crushed

1 red pepper, seeded and thinly sliced

100 g (3½ oz) baby corn, sliced diagonally

100 g (3½ oz) shiitake mushrooms, sliced

1.7 litres (3 pints) vegetable stock

3 tbsp light soy sauce

3 tbsp medium dry sherry

2 spring onions, very thinly sliced

55 g (2 oz) watercress, roughly chopped

85 g (3 oz) bean sprouts

250 g (8½ oz) smoked tofu with almonds and sesame seeds, cubed

Preparation time: 15 minutes
Cooking time: 10 minutes

Each serving provides Ⓥ

kcal 346, protein 13 g, fat 13 g (of which saturated fat 2 g), carbohydrate 41 g (of which sugars 5 g), fibre 3 g

✓✓✓	A, C, E, calcium
✓✓	copper, iron
✓	B₁, B₆, folate, niacin, zinc

1 Bring a large pan of water to the boil, add the noodles and boil for 5 minutes or until softened. When they are ready, drain them well.

2 While the noodles are cooking, heat the oil in another large saucepan. Add the ginger and garlic, and cook, stirring frequently, for about 1 minute. Add the red pepper, baby corn and shiitake mushrooms, and cook for a further 3 minutes, stirring frequently, until the vegetables are softened.

3 Pour in the vegetable stock and add the soy sauce and sherry. Bring to the boil and simmer for 3 minutes. Stir in the spring onions, watercress, bean sprouts and tofu, and cook for about 1 minute more or until the bean sprouts soften slightly.

4 Divide the noodles among 4 large serving bowls. Ladle the vegetables and soup on top and serve immediately.

Another idea

• To make scented Thai noodles with prawns and lemongrass, cook 150 g (5½ oz) cellophane noodles in boiling water for about 3 minutes or until softened. Meanwhile, stir-fry 1 tbsp grated fresh root ginger, 1 tbsp finely chopped lemongrass and 2 crushed garlic cloves in 1 tbsp sunflower oil for 1 minute. Add 1 seeded and sliced red pepper and 100 g (3½ oz) sugarsnap peas, and cook for a further 3 minutes. Pour in 1.7 litres (3 pints) vegetable stock together with 3 tbsp each light soy sauce and dry sherry. Bring to the boil and simmer for 3 minutes. Add 300 g (10½ oz) raw tiger prawns, peeled, 115 g (4 oz) baby spinach leaves, 150 g (5½ oz) bean sprouts, 4 thinly sliced spring onions and 2 tbsp chopped fresh coriander. Simmer until the prawns change from grey-blue to pink, then remove from the heat and stir in the grated zest and juice of 2 limes and 2 tbsp fish sauce. Put the drained noodles in serving bowls, ladle over the soup and serve.

Plus points

• Soba are Japan's most popular noodles. They are made from buckwheat, which though eaten as a cereal is actually the fruit of a plant related to rhubarb. Buckwheat is a good source of B vitamins and contains some calcium.

• Tofu is a good source of non-animal protein and offers good amounts of iron and B vitamins as well as useful amounts of calcium. It is low in saturated fat.

Mushroom and herb omelette

An omelette is the ultimate impromptu meal, prepared quickly and easily from a few simple ingredients. Here the classic French fines herbes *version, with fresh chervil, chives and tarragon, is made even more delicious by filling it with garlicky mushrooms. Serve with a crisp green salad and warm, crusty French bread.*

Serves 1

2 large eggs
1 tsp chopped fresh chervil
1 tsp chopped fresh tarragon
1 tsp snipped fresh chives
55 g (2 oz) mushrooms, sliced
1 garlic clove, crushed
15 g (½ oz) unsalted butter
salt and pepper

Preparation time: 5 minutes
Cooking time: 10 minutes

Each serving provides Ⓥ
kcal 314, **protein** 18 g, **fat** 27 g (of which saturated fat 12 g), **carbohydrate** 1 g (of which sugars 0.2 g), **fibre** 1 g

✓✓✓ A, B₁₂, E, copper

✓✓ B₂, niacin, selenium, zinc

✓ B₁, B₆, folate, calcium, iron, potassium

1 Crack the eggs into a bowl, then add the chervil, tarragon, chives, 1 tbsp water and salt and pepper to taste. Beat just enough to break up the eggs – take care not to overbeat, as this will spoil the texture of the omelette. Set on one side while preparing the mushrooms.

2 Heat an 18 cm (7 in) omelette or non-stick frying pan. Add the sliced mushrooms and garlic, and cook gently for 3–4 minutes or until the mushrooms have softened and released their juices. Turn up the heat a little and continue cooking for a further minute or until the mushroom juices have evaporated. Tip the mushrooms into a small bowl and set aside. Wipe the pan clean with kitchen paper.

3 Heat the pan over a high heat for a few seconds until hot. Add the butter and melt it, tilting the pan to coat the bottom. Pour in the egg and herb mixture. Cook for about 1 minute, stirring gently with a wooden spatula and pulling the cooked egg from the edge towards the centre to let the liquid egg flow onto the pan.

4 When the omelette holds together, stop stirring and cook for a further 30 seconds or until the underside is golden brown. The top surface should be just setting.

5 Scatter the mushrooms along the middle third of the omelette. Using the spatula, fold an outside third of the omelette into the centre, over the mushrooms, then fold the opposite third over that. Quickly slide the folded omelette onto a warmed plate and serve immediately.

Plus points

● Eggs have a lot to offer, in addition to being a cheap source of low-fat protein. They contain useful amounts of vitamins A, B₂, B₁₂, niacin and E, and also offer iron and zinc. There is no significant difference in nutritional content between white and brown eggs.

● Chives are mild-flavoured miniature versions of the onion, but the bulb is so small that only the green shoots are used in cooking. They are believed to stimulate the appetite and have tonic properties.

lunches for all occasions

Some more ideas

• For a spinach omelette with Parma ham crisps, beat the eggs with salt and pepper to taste. Heat the omelette pan until hot, and add 30 g (1 oz) Parma ham, trimmed of fat and cut into strips. Fry for 3–4 minutes, turning once, until crisp. Remove from the pan and set aside. Add 15 g (½ oz) butter to the pan and, when melted, cook 85 g (3 oz) baby spinach leaves briefly until wilted. Pour over the egg mixture

and cook the omelette as in the main recipe. Roll up or fold into thirds and serve topped with the Parma ham crisps.

• To make a tomato and basil soufflé omelette, separate the eggs and beat the yolks with 1 tsp water, 4 seeded and chopped plum tomatoes, 2 tbsp torn fresh basil leaves, and salt and pepper to taste. Whisk the egg whites until stiff. Stir a spoonful into the egg yolk and tomato mixture, then carefully fold in the rest of the

whites with a metal spoon. Preheat the grill to moderate. Melt 15 g (½ oz) butter in the omelette pan and pour in the egg and tomato mixture. Cook over a low heat for 2–3 minutes or until the underside of the omelette is lightly browned. Place the pan under the grill and cook for a further 2–3 minutes or until the top is golden brown and puffed up. Carefully fold the omelette in half, then slide onto a warmed plate and serve immediately.

Stir-fry pork with Chinese greens

Stir-fries do not have to be complicated, with numerous ingredients, as this simple recipe shows. Here strips of pork fillet are briefly marinated, then stir-fried with green vegetables. Nutritious egg noodles make the perfect accompaniment, turning this delicious combination into a complete meal.

Serves 4

300 g (10½ oz) pork fillet (tenderloin)
3 tbsp dry sherry
4 tsp toasted sesame oil
1 tbsp light soy sauce
1 bunch spring onions
200 g (7 oz) mange-tout
340 g (12 oz) pak choy
250 g (8½ oz) medium Chinese egg noodles
1 tbsp groundnut oil

Preparation time: 15 minutes
Cooking time: 6–7 minutes

Each serving provides

kcal 437, **protein** 28 g, **fat** 14 g (of which saturated fat 2.5 g), **carbohydrate** 50 g (of which sugars 5 g), **fibre** 5 g

✓✓✓	C
✓✓	folate
✓	A, B₁, B₆, E, niacin, calcium, copper, iron, potassium, zinc

1 Trim any excess fat from the pork and cut it across into 5 mm (¼ in) slices, then cut each slice into 5 mm (¼ in) strips. Put the pork strips into a bowl with the sherry, 1 tsp of the sesame oil and the soy sauce. Toss to mix well, then set aside to marinate while preparing the vegetables.

2 Cut the spring onions across in half, then into shreds lengthways. Halve the mange-tout lengthways. Trim the pak choy and tear into large bite-sized pieces.

3 Bring a large pan of water to the boil. Add the egg noodles and stir, then cover the pan, lower the heat and simmer for about 3 minutes, or according to the instructions on the packet, until the noodles are tender.

4 Meanwhile, heat a wok or large frying pan until hot, then add the groundnut oil and swirl it around. Add the pork strips, reserving the marinade, and stir-fry over a high heat for 3 minutes or until the meat is lightly browned and tender. Remove from the wok and set aside.

5 Add the mange-tout to the wok and stir-fry for 30 seconds, then add the spring onions and pak choy, and stir-fry for a further 1 minute. Return the pork to the wok, together with the reserved marinade, and stir-fry all together for

another 1–2 minutes or until everything is piping hot. The pak choy should have wilted, but still be a bit crisp.

6 Drain the noodles well and toss with the remaining 3 tsp sesame oil. Spoon onto warmed serving plates. Divide the stir-fried pork and greens among the plates and serve.

Plus points

• Pork contains large amounts of B-group vitamins, as well as zinc, phosphorus and iron. The iron is in the haem form, which is easily absorbed by the body.

• Pak choy, a variety of Chinese cabbage or greens, has broad white stalks topped with large, dark green leaves. Like other dark green, leafy vegetables, it is a particularly good source of folate, a B vitamin that may help to protect against heart disease.

Some more ideas

● Instead of pork, use strips of chicken or tender beef steak.

● For a vegetable stir-fry with rice noodles, mix together 1 seeded and finely chopped fresh red chilli, 2 tsp grated fresh root ginger, 1 tbsp fish sauce, 1 tbsp lime juice, 2 tsp soft dark brown sugar, 2 tsp toasted sesame oil and 3 tbsp vegetable stock or water in a small jug. Heat a wok or large frying pan, then add 1 tbsp groundnut oil. Add 200 g (7 oz) broccoli florets and 125 g (4½ oz) tiny button mushrooms and stir-fry for 2 minutes. Add 125 g (4½ oz) thin asparagus tips and stir-fry for 2 minutes. Add the sauce mixture from the jug and stir well. Finally, add 125 g (4½ oz) shredded Chinese leaves and 55 g (2 oz) cashew nuts. Stir-fry for about 3 minutes or until the sauce is thickened and bubbling and the vegetables are tender. While the vegetables are cooking, put 250 g (8½ oz) rice noodles in a bowl and cover with boiling water or stock. Stir with a fork and leave to rehydrate for 3–4 minutes or according to the packet instructions. Drain in a sieve, rinse with boiling water and drain again. Sprinkle 3 tbsp chopped fresh coriander over the vegetable stir-fry, and serve with the noodles.

Home-style potato cakes with baked beef tomatoes

Potato and leek cakes, flavoured with tasty cheese and fresh herbs, make a satisfying vegetarian meal served with big baked tomatoes and accompanied by a simple leaf salad. Use a floury, main-crop potato, such as King Edward, Desirée or Maris Piper, and mature Cheddar or another hard grating cheese with plenty of flavour.

lunches for all occasions

Serves 4

900 g (2 lb) floury potatoes, scrubbed

1 large leek, about 225 g (8 oz), sliced

2 tbsp semi-skimmed milk

2 tsp wholegrain mustard

85 g (3 oz) mature Cheddar cheese, grated

5 tbsp chopped parsley

1 tbsp chopped fresh thyme

plain flour for shaping

1 egg, beaten

85 g (3 oz) fresh wholemeal breadcrumbs

4 large beefsteak tomatoes, halved

2 tbsp garlic-flavoured olive oil

Preparation time: 35 minutes, plus cooling

Cooking time: 25 minutes

Each serving provides ⓥ

kcal 421, **protein** 17 g, **fat** 17 g (of which saturated fat 6 g), **carbohydrate** 55 g (of which sugars 8 g), **fibre** 7 g

✓✓✓	A, B₁, B₆, C, E
✓✓	folate, niacin, calcium, copper, potassium, zinc
✓	B₂, B₁₂, iron, selenium

1 Cut any large potatoes into halves or quarters. Bring a large pan of water to the boil and add the potatoes. Bring back to the boil, then turn down the heat and cook for 15 minutes or until tender. Add the leek to the pan for the last 5 minutes of the cooking time.

2 Drain the vegetables thoroughly, then spread them out on a tray and leave them to cool. Preheat the oven to 220°C (425°F, gas mark 7).

3 When the potatoes are cool enough to handle, peel them and put in a large bowl with the leek. Crush the potatoes with a fork. Add the milk, mustard, cheese, parsley and thyme, and mix well together.

4 Divide the mixture into 8 portions. Shape each into a rough ball, then press on a floured surface into a flat cake about 9 cm (3½ in) across and 3 cm (1¼ in) thick.

5 Set the potato cakes on a clean tray or platter. Brush with the beaten egg and sprinkle over half the breadcrumbs. Turn the potato cakes over and coat the other sides with egg and breadcrumbs. Transfer the potato cakes to a lightly greased, non-stick baking sheet and bake for 15 minutes.

6 Meanwhile, place the tomatoes in an ovenproof dish, cut side up. Brush with the garlic oil and sprinkle over any remaining breadcrumbs.

7 Turn the potato cakes over carefully with a flat fish slice or palette knife. Put the tomatoes into the oven with the potato cakes and bake for a further 10 minutes or until the potato cakes are golden. Serve hot.

Plus points

• Potatoes are a valuable source of starchy carbohydrates for everyday meals. They can also be a useful source of vitamin C – not so much because of the amount of this vitamin in the potato, but because of the quantity of potatoes that are eaten. Cooking potatoes in their skins and then peeling them afterwards helps to preserve the vitamin content.

• Potato cakes are often fried in oil or butter. Here they are baked to produce cakes that are equally tasty but with a lower fat content.

Another idea

● Make rosti-style potato and spinach cakes. Use 675 g (1½ lb) potatoes and cook them, unpeeled, in boiling water for just 8 minutes. Drain and cool. Meanwhile, soften 1 chopped onion in 1 tbsp sunflower oil for 2 minutes. Add 1 tbsp chopped fresh root ginger, 1 tbsp cumin seeds and 1 tbsp medium hot curry paste, and cook gently for a further 1 minute, stirring constantly. Add 225 g (8 oz) baby spinach leaves and 3 tbsp water, and cook gently for 3 minutes or until the spinach has wilted. Tip the mixture into a large bowl. Peel the cooled potatoes and grate them into the bowl. Add 3 tbsp chopped fresh coriander, and season with salt and pepper to taste. Use 2 forks to mix together. Heap the mixture in 8 mounds on lightly oiled baking sheets and press down flat. Bake in a preheated 220ºC (425ºF, gas mark 7) oven for 15 minutes, then turn the cakes over and bake for a further 10 minutes. Serve with a minty yogurt raita, made by mixing 150 g (5½ oz) plain low-fat yogurt with ¼ cucumber, finely diced, and 1 tsp concentrated mint sauce.

Smoked haddock hash

This smoked haddock and potato hash, subtly flavoured with curry powder, is a very easy dish to make and is ideal for lunch when you want something warming and filling. The Savoy cabbage adds crunch and extra vitamins. It only needs a mixed leaf salad or sliced tomatoes to make a well-balanced meal.

Serves 4

900 g (2 lb) floury potatoes, peeled and cut
    into 5 mm (¼ in) cubes

2 tsp curry powder

2 tbsp sunflower oil

300 ml (10 fl oz) fish or vegetable stock

300 g (10½ oz) piece of smoked haddock
    fillet

1 bunch spring onions, chopped

115 g (4 oz) Savoy cabbage, finely shredded

3 tbsp chopped fresh flat-leaf parsley

4 tbsp Greek-style yogurt

salt and pepper

sprigs of fresh flat-leaf parsley to garnish

Preparation time: 20 minutes
Cooking time: 30 minutes

Each serving provides

kcal 346, **protein** 23 g, **fat** 10 g (of which saturated fat 3 g), **carbohydrate** 44 g (of which sugars 6 g), **fibre** 5 g

✓✓✓ B_6, B_{12}, C, E

✓✓ B_1, folate, niacin, potassium, selenium

✓   A, B_2, calcium, copper, iron, zinc

1 Put the potatoes into a bowl. Add the curry powder and toss to coat the potatoes evenly all over. Heat the oil in a large non-stick frying pan, add the potatoes and fry over a moderate heat for 20 minutes, turning occasionally.

2 Meanwhile, pour the stock into a second frying pan and bring to the boil. Reduce the heat, then add the smoked haddock. Cover the pan and simmer very gently for 8–10 minutes or until the fish will flake easily. Remove the fish from the pan using a fish slice and place on a plate. Flake the flesh, discarding any skin and bones. Set aside. Discard the stock.

3 Add the spring onions and cabbage to the potatoes and fry, stirring frequently, for a further 3–5 minutes or until the potatoes are cooked and crisp and the cabbage is wilted.

4 Stir in the smoked haddock, chopped parsley and yogurt, and season with salt and pepper to taste. Continue cooking gently until piping hot, stirring occasionally. Serve hot, garnished with parsley sprigs.

Some more ideas

● Use sweet potatoes in place of the white potatoes.

● Instead of flat-leaf parsley, use 1–2 tbsp chopped fresh coriander or tarragon.

● For a salmon hash with broccoli and peas, use salmon fillet in place of the smoked haddock. Cook the potatoes as in the main recipe, but omit the curry powder. Meanwhile, steam 170 g (6 oz) broccoli florets and cook 140 g (5 oz) frozen peas until tender. Add the broccoli and peas to the potatoes together with the flaked salmon, yogurt and 2 tbsp each chopped parsley and snipped fresh chives.

Plus points

● Smoked haddock is an excellent source of protein while having a low fat content. As a sea fish it is also a particularly good and reliable source of iodine, a mineral needed for synthesis of thyroid hormones, which have many diverse and important functions in the body.

● Savoy cabbage, easily recognisable by its firm, dark green, crinkly leaves, contains flavonoids that are believed to help suppress cancer-causing cells. Savoy cabbage also provides other nutrients with protective properties, including vitamins C and E.

Chicken and cashew pancakes

Chicken stir-fried with carrots, celery and cabbage, then lightly flavoured with orange and sesame, makes a delicious filling for pancakes. This dish is sure to meet with your family's approval.

lunches for all occasions

Serves 4

115 g (4 oz) plain flour

1 egg, beaten

300 ml (10 fl oz) semi-skimmed milk

1 tsp sunflower oil

salt and pepper

Chicken and cashew nut filling

55 g (2 oz) cashew nuts

1 tbsp sunflower oil

300 g (10½ oz) skinless boneless chicken breasts (fillets), cut into strips

1 garlic clove, crushed

1 tsp finely chopped fresh root ginger

1 fresh red chilli, seeded and finely chopped (optional)

2 carrots, cut into thin sticks

2 celery sticks, cut into thin sticks

grated zest of ½ orange

200 g (7 oz) Savoy cabbage, shredded

1 tbsp light soy sauce, plus extra for serving

1 tsp toasted sesame oil

Preparation time: 15–20 minutes
Cooking time: about 30 minutes

Each serving provides

kcal 384, **protein** 29 g, **fat** 15 g (of which saturated fat 3 g), **carbohydrate** 35 g (of which sugars 10 g), **fibre** 4 g

✓✓✓	A, E, niacin
✓✓	B₁, B₆, C, folate, calcium, copper, potassium, selenium, zinc
✓	B₂, B₁₂, iron

1 To make the pancakes, sift the flour into a bowl and add a little salt and pepper to taste. Make a well in the centre. Mix the egg with the milk, then pour into the well. Gradually whisk the flour into the egg and milk to form a smooth batter.

2 Use a little of the oil to lightly grease a 20 cm (8 in) non-stick pancake pan, and place it on a moderate heat. Pour in a little of the batter and swirl it evenly across the surface, then cook for 2 minutes to form a pancake. Toss the pancake or flip it over with a palette knife and cook on the other side for about 30 seconds. Slide out onto a warm heatproof plate and cover with a sheet of greaseproof paper.

3 Cook the remaining batter in the same way, making 8 pancakes in all and stacking them up, interleaved with greaseproof paper. Grease the pan with more oil between pancakes as necessary. When all the pancakes have been made, cover the pancake stack with foil, sealing it well. Place the plate over a pan of gently simmering water to keep the pancakes warm while you prepare the filling.

4 Heat a wok or large frying pan. Add the cashew nuts and stir-fry them over a moderate heat for a few minutes or until golden. Remove to a plate and set aside.

5 Add the oil to the wok or frying pan and swirl it around, then add the chicken, garlic, ginger and chilli, if using. Stir-fry for 3 minutes.

6 Add the carrot and celery sticks, and stir-fry for a further 2 minutes. Add the orange zest and cabbage, and stir-fry for 1 minute. Sprinkle over the soy sauce and sesame oil, and stir-fry for another minute. Return the cashews to the pan and toss to mix with the other ingredients.

7 Divide the stir-fry filling among the warm pancakes and fold them over or roll up. Serve immediately, with a little extra soy sauce to sprinkle.

Plus points

● Cashew nuts are a rich source of protein, fibre, and minerals such as iron, magnesium and selenium. Though cashews are high in fat, the majority of it is the 'healthy' monounsaturated type.

● Stir-frying is a healthy way to cook, because only a little oil is needed, any meat or poultry used is very lean, and cooking is done quickly over quite a high heat so that the maximum amount of nutrients in the vegetables is retained.

Some more ideas

- Add 2 tsp finely chopped fresh root ginger and the grated zest of 1 orange to the pancake batter.
- For speed, use bought ready-made pancakes, or Chinese pancakes as served with Peking duck. Allow 3 Chinese pancakes per serving.

- To make sesame duck pancakes, stir-fry 300 g (10½ oz) skinless, sliced duck breast with 1 crushed garlic clove and 2 tsp finely chopped fresh root ginger in 1 tbsp sunflower oil for 3–4 minutes. Add 1 tbsp dry sherry, 1 tbsp dark soy sauce and 1 tsp clear honey and stir, then add 150 g (5½ oz) bean sprouts

and toss to mix. While the duck is cooking, blanch 85 g (3 oz) fine Chinese egg noodles in boiling water for 2–3 minutes; drain and add to the stir-fry with 1 tsp toasted sesame oil and 6 shredded spring onions. Toss together until piping hot, then divide the stir-fry among the pancakes and roll up or fold over.

Thai coconut rice with prawns

This aromatic seafood and rice dish, combining the classic Thai flavourings of coconut, lime and ginger, makes a very tempting lunch. Thai jasmine rice is a naturally fragrant rice with a delicate flavour. If you do not have any in your storecupboard, basmati rice makes a good substitute.

Serves 4

600 ml (1 pint) fish stock
200 g (7 oz) Thai jasmine rice
1½ tbsp sunflower oil
1 garlic clove, finely chopped
2.5 cm (1 in) piece fresh root ginger, finely chopped
1 bunch spring onions, thinly sliced
250 g (8½ oz) broccoli florets, thinly sliced
12 raw tiger prawns, peeled but tails left on
juice of 1 lime
1 tsp fish sauce
3 tbsp chopped fresh coriander
90 ml (3 fl oz) coconut milk
salt and pepper

To garnish

curls of toasted fresh coconut (optional)
lime wedges

Preparation time: 15 minutes
Cooking time: 16–18 minutes

Each serving provides

kcal 300, protein 18 g, fat 6 g (of which saturated fat 1 g), carbohydrate 44 g (of which sugars 3 g), fibre 2 g

✓✓✓ B_{12}, C, E
✓ A, folate, niacin, calcium, copper, iron, potassium, selenium, zinc

1 Bring the stock to the boil in a large saucepan. Add the rice, then cover and simmer for 10–12 minutes or until the rice is just tender.

2 Meanwhile, heat a wok or large frying pan, add the oil and swirl it around. Add the garlic, ginger and spring onions, and stir-fry for 1 minute. Add the broccoli and stir-fry for a further 2 minutes, then add the prawns and stir-fry for 2–3 minutes or until the prawns change from a grey-blue colour to pink.

3 Stir in the lime juice and fish sauce and stir-fry for 30 seconds, then add the coriander and salt and pepper to taste. Toss to mix.

4 Add the coconut milk to the rice and mix well. Spoon the rice onto a serving platter or individual plates, top with the sitr-fried prawns and garnish with curls of coconut, if using, and lime wedges. Serve immediately.

Some more ideas

• For a lower-fat dish, simmer the garlic, ginger and onions in 2–3 tbsp extra stock to soften instead of frying in oil, and reduce the amount of coconut milk to 2 tbsp.

• Add 8 baby corn with the broccoli.

• To make tropical chicken rice, replace the prawns with 300 g (10½ oz) skinless boneless chicken breast (fillet), cut into thin strips. Instead of broccoli use 1 seeded and diced green pepper, and stir-fry with the chicken for 5–6 minutes. Peel, stone and dice a medium-sized mango and stir into the chicken mixture with the lime juice (omit the fish sauce).

Plus points

• Rice is a very good source of starchy carbohydrate. Because it is easy and quick to cook, it is a great choice for anyone with a busy lifestyle.

• Prawns are a low-fat, high-protein food. They are an excellent source of vitamin B_{12}, essential for the formation of red blood cells and the maintenance of a healthy nervous system. Prawns are also an excellent source of selenium, an important antioxidant.

• Lime juice accentuates flavours, reducing the need for salt, and adds an extra boost of vitamin C to a dish.

Baked rigatoni with aubergine

Aubergine adds a lovely flavour and texture to this hearty vegetarian pasta dish that is topped with a crisp layer of breadcrumbs and Parmesan. The rich tomato sauce could be made in advance, then the dish can be quickly assembled and baked when you wish. Serve with a green side salad.

Serves 4

2 tbsp extra virgin olive oil
1 large onion, chopped
2 garlic cloves, crushed
4 tbsp red wine
2 cans chopped tomatoes in rich tomato juice, about 400 g each
5 sun-dried tomatoes packed in oil, about 45 g (1½ oz) in total, drained and chopped
1 aubergine, cut into 1 cm (½ in) cubes
2 tbsp chopped fresh oregano
225 g (8 oz) rigatoni or other chunky pasta tube shapes, such as penne
30 g (1 oz) fresh Granary breadcrumbs
30 g (1 oz) Parmesan cheese, freshly grated
salt and pepper

Preparation time: 35 minutes
Cooking time: 15–20 minutes

1 Heat the oil in a large saucepan, add the onion and cook gently for 4–5 minutes, stirring frequently, until it has softened and turned lightly golden. Add the garlic and cook gently for a further 1–2 minutes.

2 Pour in the wine and allow it to bubble for a few minutes, then add the canned tomatoes with their juice, the sun-dried tomatoes, aubergine and oregano. Bring to the boil, then reduce the heat, cover and simmer gently for 15–20 minutes, stirring occasionally.

3 Meanwhile, cook the pasta in a large pan of boiling water for 10–12 minutes, or according to the packet instructions, until al dente. Drain well.

4 Preheat the oven to 200ºC (400ºF, gas mark 6). Season the tomato sauce with salt and pepper to taste. Tip the cooked pasta into a large, lightly greased ovenproof dish. Pour over the sauce and mix well together so that all the pasta is coated.

5 Combine the breadcrumbs and Parmesan in a bowl, and sprinkle this mixture evenly over the top of the pasta. Bake for 15–20 minutes or until the sauce is bubbling and the top is golden brown and crisp. Serve hot.

Plus points

- Pasta is a versatile starchy carbohydrate food, providing protein, fibre (particularly if wholemeal varieties are used), B vitamins and minerals. It is also low in fat – it is the fattening sauces often served with pasta that push up the calorie and fat content of a dish.
- Although aubergines are low in calories, dishes using them tend to be high in fat, as the aubergines are often fried in oil, which they soak up. Cooking them in tomato juice is a clever and low-fat way to soften them, while adding additional flavour.

Each serving provides   ⓥ

kcal 425, **protein** 14 g, **fat** 15 g (of which saturated fat 3 g), **carbohydrate** 59 g (of which sugars 12 g), **fibre** 6 g

✓✓✓	E
✓✓	B₁, C, niacin, copper, potassium, zinc
✓	A, B₆, folate, calcium, iron, selenium

Another idea

• For a mushroom and spinach pasta bake, combine 500 g (1 lb 2 oz) chopped or sliced mushrooms, 1 small chopped onion, 500 ml (17 fl oz) vegetable stock, 150 ml (5 fl oz) dry white wine and about 10 chopped fresh sage leaves in a saucepan. Bring to the boil, then cover and simmer for 5 minutes. Drain the mushrooms, reserving the cooking liquid. Mix 2 tbsp cornflour with 5 tbsp semi-skimmed milk, and gradually stir in the reserved cooking liquid. Pour this mixture back into the saucepan and heat gently, stirring, until thickened. Stir in 3 tbsp crème fraîche, 1 tsp wholegrain mustard and salt and pepper to taste. Add the cooked mushrooms and 150 g (5½ oz) baby spinach leaves. Warm gently so the spinach just wilts. Meanwhile, cook 225 g (8 oz) rigatoni or penne in boiling water for 10–12 minutes, or according to the packet instructions, until al dente. Drain and tip into a greased ovenproof dish. Pour over the spinach and mushroom sauce and stir to combine. Lightly toast 2 thick slices of multigrain wholemeal bread, remove the crusts and cut into cubes. Scatter these over the pasta together with 30 g (1 oz) freshly grated Parmesan cheese. Bake in a preheated 200ºC (400ºF, gas mark 6) oven for 15 minutes or until the sauce is bubbling. Garnish with fresh sage leaves and serve hot.

Cheese and watercress soufflé

Soufflés have a quite undeserved reputation for being difficult to make. This tasty soufflé is, in fact, very quick and easy to prepare and makes a satisfying lunch when served with crusty bread and a side salad.

Serves 4

1 tsp butter
15 g (½ oz) Parmesan cheese, freshly grated
15 g (½ oz) fine dry breadcrumbs
85 g (3 oz) watercress
3 tbsp cornflour
300 ml (10 fl oz) semi-skimmed milk
4 eggs, separated
1 tbsp wholegrain mustard
85 g (3 oz) Gruyère cheese, grated
salt and pepper

Preparation time: 20 minutes
Cooking time: 30–35 minutes

Each serving provides   Ⓥ

kcal 293, protein 19 g, fat 18 g (of which saturated fat 8 g), carbohydrate 16 g (of which sugars 4 g), fibre 1 g

✓✓✓	A, B₁₂, niacin, calcium
✓✓	E, niacin, zinc
✓	B₂, C, folate, copper, iron, selenium

1 Preheat the oven to 200°C (400°F, gas mark 6). Lightly butter the inside of a 1.5 litre (2¾ pint) soufflé dish. Mix together the Parmesan and breadcrumbs, and sprinkle half of this mixture over the bottom and sides of the dish, turning and tilting the dish to coat evenly. Set aside.

2 Remove the thicker stalks from the watercress and discard. Finely chop the rest of the watercress and set aside.

3 Mix the cornflour with a little of the milk to make a smooth paste. Heat the rest of the milk until almost boiling, then pour onto the cornflour mixture, stirring constantly. Return to the pan and stir over a moderate heat until the sauce thickens and is smooth.

4 Remove from the heat and add the egg yolks, beating them thoroughly into the sauce. Stir in the chopped watercress, mustard, Gruyère cheese, and salt and pepper to taste.

5 In a clean, dry bowl, whisk the egg whites until they will hold soft peaks. Fold one-quarter of the whites into the sauce mixture to lighten it, then gently fold in the rest of the whites.

6 Spoon the mixture into the prepared soufflé dish and sprinkle the top with the remaining Parmesan and breadcrumb mixture. Bake the soufflé for 30–35 minutes or until well risen and golden brown. Serve immediately.

Some more ideas

● Instead of Gruyère, use a blue cheese such as Gorgonzola, Stilton or Danish blue.

● Try a Greek-style feta and watercress soufflé, replacing the Gruyère cheese with 75 g (2½ oz) crumbled feta. Sprinkle the soufflé with a pinch of freshly grated nutmeg before serving.

● For a smoked haddock and spinach soufflé, use 85 g (3 oz) smoked haddock fillet and 85 g (3 oz) fresh spinach leaves. Cook the haddock gently in the milk for 5–6 minutes, then drain, reserving the milk for the sauce. Flake the haddock, discarding any skin and bones. Wash the spinach, then cook for 2–3 minutes, with just the water clinging to the leaves, until wilted. Drain well, squeezing out excess moisture, then chop the spinach. Add the haddock and spinach to the sauce in step 4, in place of the Gruyère and watercress.

Plus points

● Gruyère cheese has a distinctive flavour and creamy, melting texture. It contributes to the protein and calcium content of this soufflé, as well as providing zinc, a mineral that has an important role to play in wound healing.

● Most soufflés are based on a mixture of butter and flour called a roux. This version uses cornflour instead, which works just as well and keeps the total fat content low.

Lentil risotto

Lentils add extra flavour and texture to this Italian-style mushroom risotto and also make it more nutritious. Serve with roasted or griddled Italian vegetables, such as peppers and courgettes, or a mixed salad, for a satisfying lunch, and one that is particularly tempting on a cold winter's day.

Serves 4

170 g (6 oz) green lentils
500 ml (17 fl oz) vegetable stock
1 tbsp extra virgin olive oil
1 onion, finely chopped
1 garlic clove, crushed
3 celery sticks, chopped
1 red pepper, seeded and diced
1 tsp ground coriander
1 tsp ground cumin
225 g (8 oz) mushrooms, sliced
170 g (6 oz) risotto rice
200 ml (7 fl oz) dry white wine
3 tbsp coarsely chopped fresh coriander,
    plus extra to garnish
50 g (1¾ oz) Parmesan cheese, cut into
    shavings
salt and pepper

Preparation time: 30 minutes
Cooking time: 45 minutes

Each serving provides

kcal 429, protein 21 g, fat 9 g (of which saturated fat 3 g), carbohydrate 59 g (of which sugars 6 g), fibre 6 g

✓✓✓	A, B$_6$, C, copper, selenium, zinc
✓✓	B$_6$, niacin, calcium, iron, potassium
✓	B$_1$, B$_2$, folate

1 Cook the lentils in a saucepan of boiling water for 20 minutes, then drain and set aside. Place the stock in the saucepan and bring to simmering point over a moderate heat. Lower the heat so the stock is simmering gently.

2 Heat the oil in another large saucepan, add the onion, garlic and celery, and cook for 5 minutes or until softened, stirring occasionally. Add the red pepper and the ground coriander and cumin, and cook for 1 minute, stirring.

3 Add the mushrooms, rice and cooked lentils and stir to mix. Pour in the wine and add a ladleful of the hot stock. Bring to a gentle boil and bubble until most of the liquid has been absorbed, stirring frequently.

4 Add another ladleful of stock and cook until it is absorbed, stirring frequently. Repeat this gradual addition of the hot stock until it has all been added. The rice should be creamy and tender but still with some bite, and the lentils cooked.

5 Stir in the chopped coriander and season with salt and pepper to taste. Serve hot, sprinkled with the Parmesan shavings and extra chopped coriander.

Some more ideas

● Instead of green lentils, use brown or Puy lentils.

● Replace the Parmesan shavings with 2 chopped hard-boiled eggs.

● Make a pearl barley 'risotto'. Soften 2 sliced leeks and 1 crushed garlic clove in 1 tbsp extra virgin olive oil. Add 1 seeded and diced red or yellow pepper, 250 g (8½ oz) pearl barley, 2 tsp dried herbes de Provence, 200 ml (7 fl oz) dry white wine and 100 ml (3½ fl oz) hot vegetable stock. Simmer for 45 minutes, gradually adding a further 400–500 ml (14–17 fl oz) hot stock and stirring frequently, until the pearl barley is cooked and tender. Meanwhile, steam 225 g (8 oz) broccoli florets and cook 170 g (6 oz) frozen peas. Stir these into the barley risotto and heat gently until piping hot. Season with salt and pepper to taste and serve, topped with the Parmesan shavings.

Plus points

● Lentils are the small seeds of a variety of leguminous plants. They are a good source of protein, starchy carbohydrate, dietary fibre and B vitamins.

● Parmesan cheese, which is made from unpasteurised skimmed cow's milk, contributes protein to this dish, as well as calcium and vitamin B$_{12}$.

lunches for all occasions

Special Bites

Finger food for celebrations

FESTIVE OCCASIONS DEMAND SUMPTUOUS and glamorous party food. Making it nutritious too is easier than you might think. Impress your guests with little Chinese dumplings presented in bamboo steaming baskets, or bake crab-filled filo triangles and serve with a dipping sauce. Shape pretty tartlet cases from bread slices and spoon in caramelised onions and walnuts, or cut a very 'deep-pan' pizza into bite-sized squares. Mini kebabs with monkfish and mussels make perfect party bites. Or what about sticky spare ribs, or crisp cheese sticks flavoured with Parmesan and sesame seeds?

Monkfish and mussel sticks

To create these succulent mini kebabs, marinated cubes of monkfish fillet and fresh mussels are threaded onto skewers with a selection of colourful vegetables, then lightly grilled. They make an extra special hot nibble to hand round at a celebration party or present on a buffet table.

Makes 16 kebabs

finely grated zest and juice of 1 lemon

juice of 1 lime

1 tbsp extra virgin olive oil

2 tsp clear honey

1 garlic clove, crushed

1 tbsp chopped fresh oregano or marjoram

1 tbsp chopped parsley

200 g (7 oz) monkfish fillet, cut into 16 small cubes

16 shelled fresh mussels, about 125 g (4½ oz) in total

1 small yellow pepper, seeded and cut into 16 small chunks

1 courgette, cut into 16 thin slices

16 cherry tomatoes

salt and pepper

lime or lemon wedges to garnish

Preparation time: 20 minutes, plus 1 hour marinating

Cooking time: 8–10 minutes

1 Put the lemon zest and juice, lime juice, oil, honey, garlic, chopped oregano or marjoram, parsley, and salt and pepper to taste in a shallow non-metallic dish. Whisk together, then add the monkfish cubes and mussels. Turn the seafood to coat all over with the marinade. Cover and marinate in the fridge for 1 hour.

2 Meanwhile, put 16 wooden skewers in warm water and leave to soak for 10 minutes. Drain. Preheat the grill to moderately high.

3 Onto each skewer, thread 1 cube of monkfish, 1 mussel, 1 piece of yellow pepper, 1 slice of courgette and a cherry tomato. (Reserve the marinade.) Leave the ends of the skewers empty so they will be easy to hold.

4 Place the kebabs on a rack in the grill pan and grill for 8–10 minutes or until the monkfish is cooked and the vegetables are just tender, turning occasionally and brushing frequently with the marinade. Serve hot, garnished with lime or lemon wedges.

Some more ideas

● For scallop and prawn sticks, use 16 shelled fresh queen scallops and 16 raw peeled prawns in place of the monkfish and mussels.

● To make tuna or swordfish sticks, cut 300 g (10½ oz) fresh tuna or swordfish fillet into 16 small cubes and marinate in a mixture of the finely grated zest and juice of 1 lime, 1 small crushed garlic clove, 1 tbsp extra virgin olive oil, 1 tsp Cajun seasoning, and salt and pepper to taste. Seed 1 red pepper and cut into 16 small chunks, and quarter 4 shallots or baby onions. Thread the marinated fish onto skewers with the prepared vegetables and 16 very small button mushrooms. Grill as in the main recipe.

Each kebab provides

kcal 30, **protein** 3 g, **fat** 1 g (of which saturated fat 0.1 g), **carbohydrate** 2 g (of which sugars 2 g), **fibre** 0.5 g

✓✓	B$_{12}$
✓	C, E

Plus points

● Monkfish has a huge, ugly head, and only the tail is eaten. The firm flesh tastes rather like lobster. Monkfish is an excellent source of phosphorus and a useful source of potassium, which is vital to help regulate blood pressure

● Mussels provide several minerals, in particular iron, zinc, copper and iodine. Mussels are also an extremely good source of vitamin B$_{12}$, needed for the maintenance of a healthy nervous system.

special bites

Gingered crab filo parcels

These Oriental-style, triangular parcels of crisp, light filo pastry enclose a ginger-flavoured filling of crab, water chestnuts and sweetcorn. They look and taste wonderful, and are really easy to make. Prepare them ahead for a party, then bake just before serving with a sweet chilli dipping sauce.

Makes 18 parcels

1 can white meat crab, about 170 g, drained

1 can water chestnuts, about 225 g, drained and coarsely chopped

1 can sweetcorn, about 200 g, drained

4 spring onions, chopped

1 tbsp finely chopped fresh root ginger

1 fresh red chilli, seeded and finely chopped

2 tbsp Chinese cooking wine or dry sherry

2 tbsp groundnut oil

1 tbsp toasted sesame oil

6 sheets filo pastry, about 50 x 30 cm (20 x 12 in) each, about 225 g (8 oz) in total

1 tbsp sesame seeds

salt and pepper

To serve

spring onions

Thai sweet chilli dipping sauce

Preparation time: 45–50 minutes

Cooking time: 12–13 minutes

Each parcel provides

kcal 79, **protein** 3 g, **fat** 3 g (of which saturated fat 0.5 g), **carbohydrate** 11 g (of which sugars 1 g), **fibre** 0.5 g

1 Preheat the oven to 200°C (400°F, gas mark 6). Combine the crab, water chestnuts, sweetcorn, spring onions, ginger, red chilli and Chinese cooking wine or sherry in a bowl, and season with salt and pepper to taste. Mix together the groundnut and sesame oils in a cup.

2 Roll up the 6 sheets of filo pastry loosely, rolling from a short side. Using a sharp knife, cut the roll across evenly into 3. Cover 2 of these shorter rolls with cling film to prevent them from drying out. Unravel the third roll, remove one of the strips and set the rest aside, covered.

3 Lay the strip of filo flat on the work surface, with a short end nearest to you, and brush with a little of the oil mixture. Place a heaped teaspoon of the crab mixture near the bottom, towards the right-hand corner of the short end, and fold the pastry diagonally over it. Continue folding diagonally, over and over, until you reach the end of the strip, making a neat triangular parcel. Place on a baking sheet, seam side down.

4 Repeat with remaining strips of filo, uncovering them only when needed, until all of the crab mixture is used. (The parcels can be prepared in advance; cover the baking sheets with cling film and keep in the fridge. The baking time may need to be increased to 15 minutes if the parcels are very cold.)

5 Lightly brush the tops of the parcels with any remaining oil mixture and sprinkle with the sesame seeds. Bake for 12–13 minutes or until crisp and golden.

6 Transfer the parcels to a wire rack and cool slightly. Meanwhile, shred the tops of the spring onions for garnishing, to form 'brushes'. Serve the parcels warm, on a tray garnished with the spring onion brushes and a little dish of Thai sweet chilli dipping sauce to accompany.

Plus points

● Using filo for these parcels keeps the fat content low. This is because only a light brushing of oil is needed to stick the pastry edges together and to give a golden brown sheen and crisp texture, and the parcels are baked rather than deep fried.

● Ginger is believed to aid digestion and help stimulate the circulation. It is also used as an antiseptic, to help relieve the symptoms of colds as well as morning and travel sickness.

Some more ideas

- For prawn filo parcels, use 125 g (4½ oz) chopped cooked peeled prawns in place of the crab meat.
- To make mini spring rolls with a vegetable filling, mix together 200 g (7 oz) bean sprouts, 1 grated carrot, 1 can sliced bamboo shoots, about 220 g, drained and chopped, 4 chopped spring onions and 125 g (4½ oz) chopped mushrooms. Heat 1 tbsp groundnut oil in a large pan, add 1 tbsp finely chopped fresh root ginger and 2 crushed garlic cloves, and stir-fry for 30 seconds. Add the vegetable mixture and stir-fry for 1 minute. Sprinkle over 1 tbsp light soy sauce and 1 tbsp Chinese cooking wine or dry sherry, and stir-fry for 1 minute, then cool.

Cut the filo pastry into strips as in the main recipe. Mix together 2 tbsp groundnut oil and 1 tbsp toasted sesame oil. Lightly brush a strip of filo with a little of the oil mixture, then place a heaped teaspoon of filling on the centre base. Fold in the sides and roll up to make a little cigar shape. Repeat with the remaining filo and filling. Finish and bake as in the main recipe.

Sticky spare ribs

Here pork spare ribs are simmered first to tenderise the meat and to remove some of the fat, before being roasted in a deliciously sticky orange and mustard glaze. Choose the meatiest ribs you can find. When serving them, remember to put out finger bowls and plenty of napkins for cleaning sticky fingers.

Makes 12 spare ribs

12 meaty pork spare ribs, about 900 g (2 lb) in total

3 tbsp red wine vinegar

2 tsp sunflower oil

large strip of orange zest

150 ml (5 fl oz) orange juice

1 tbsp tomato purée

2 tbsp dark soft brown sugar

2 tbsp Worcestershire sauce

1 tbsp French mustard

½–1 tsp chilli powder, or to taste

Preparation time: 30 minutes
Cooking time: 40–45 minutes

1 Preheat the oven to 200°C (400°F, gas mark 6). Trim as much fat as possible off the spare ribs, then put them in a saucepan. Cover with cold water and add 2 tbsp of the vinegar. Bring to the boil, then simmer for 20 minutes, skimming the surface from time to time.

2 Meanwhile, combine the remaining 1 tbsp vinegar, the oil, orange zest and juice, tomato purée, brown sugar, Worcestershire sauce, mustard and chilli powder in a small pan and bring to the boil. Simmer for 4–5 minutes or until slightly reduced.

3 Drain the ribs and arrange them in a single layer in a large roasting tin. Pour over the orange mixture and turn the ribs to coat them evenly. Loosely cover with foil and roast for 20 minutes.

4 Remove the foil and roast for a further 20–25 minutes, turning and basting occasionally, until the ribs are dark brown and sticky. Transfer to a large serving dish and serve warm.

Some more ideas

• For Oriental spare ribs, make the glaze from 2 tsp grated fresh root ginger, 3 tbsp clear honey, 1 tbsp tomato purée, 2 tbsp dark soy sauce, 2 tbsp rice wine or dry sherry, 2 tbsp hoisin sauce, 2 tsp sherry vinegar and 1 tsp chilli sauce.

• Try a Cajun dry rub instead of a glaze. Mix together 2 tbsp paprika, 2 tsp ground cumin, 1 tsp dried thyme, ¼ tsp black pepper, ½ tsp cayenne pepper and 2 finely chopped garlic cloves. Simmer the ribs as in the main recipe, then drain, cool slightly and coat in the rub before roasting.

Each spare rib provides

kcal 90, **protein** 7.5 g, **fat** 4 g (of which saturated fat 1 g), **carbohydrate** 6 g (of which sugars 6 g), **fibre** 0.1 g

✓ B_1, B_6, B_{12}, E, niacin, calcium, zinc

Plus points

• Pork has an undeserved reputation for being a fatty meat – modern pork is extremely lean due to changes in breeding practices and butchery techniques. The fat that is still present is higher in mono and polyunsaturated fats than in saturated fats.

• Spare ribs are one of the fattier cuts of pork. Trimming off any visible fat, simmering in water and then roasting until crisp are clever ways to reduce their fat content.

special bites

Caramelised onion tartlets

Croustades – made from thin slices of bread pushed into bun tins, brushed with melted butter and baked to crisp – are a great alternative to pastry for savoury tartlets. These are filled with a mixture of onions and sun-dried tomatoes. Both the croustades and filling can be prepared ahead, then warmed and assembled for serving.

Makes 12 tartlets

30 g (1 oz) butter, melted

12 thin slices white bread

1 tbsp extra virgin olive oil

2 large onions, about 450 g (1 lb) in total, thinly sliced

30 g (1 oz) sun-dried tomatoes packed in oil, drained and roughly chopped

2 tsp finely chopped fresh thyme

30 g (1 oz) walnut pieces

salt and pepper

Preparation time: 20 minutes

Cooking time: 35 minutes

1 Preheat the oven to 230°C (450°F, gas mark 8). Lightly brush 12 deep bun tins with a little of the melted butter. Using a 7.5 cm (3 in) pastry cutter, cut a disc from each slice of bread. Flatten each bread disc with a rolling pin, then press into the buttered bun tins to line them evenly, curving the edge of the bread slightly to make large scallop shapes.

2 Brush the bread cases with the rest of the melted butter and bake for 8–10 minutes or until crisp and golden. Set aside in a warm place until ready to fill. (If made ahead, keep the bread cases in an airtight tin.)

3 Heat the oil in a large heavy pan with a well-fitting lid. Add the onions and stir well. Cover with the lid and cook over a low heat for 20 minutes or until the onions are very soft.

4 Remove the lid, turn up the heat and cook rapidly, stirring, until the onions turn a dark golden brown. Remove from the heat and stir in the sun-dried tomatoes and thyme. Season with salt and pepper to taste. (If made ahead, cool the filling and keep in the fridge, then reheat just before filling the bread cases.)

5 Divide the onion filling among the croustades, then scatter the chopped walnuts over the top. Serve hot.

Some more ideas

● Use filo pastry cases instead of croustades. Brush the bun tins with melted butter, then cut 270 g (9½ oz) filo pastry into 9 cm (3½ in) squares (you will need 48 squares). Press 4 squares, at different angles, into each bun tin, then brush with the rest of the melted butter. Bake in a preheated 220°C (425°F, gas mark 7) oven for 4–5 minutes or until crisp and golden.

● For ratatouille tartlets, soften 1 finely chopped onion in 1 tbsp extra virgin olive oil, then stir in 2 chopped garlic cloves and 1 small red pepper, seeded and finely diced. Cook, stirring frequently, for 2 minutes. Add 1 small aubergine and 1 courgette, both cut into small dice. Cook for 1 minute, then add 55 g (2 oz) finely chopped sun-dried tomatoes and 1 tsp chopped fresh thyme. Stir, then cover tightly and cook gently for 15–20 minutes or until the vegetables are tender. Season, then divide among the warm bread cases. Scatter over 30 g (1 oz) toasted pine nuts and serve.

Plus point

● Eating walnuts in moderate but regular amounts may help to reduce blood cholesterol levels and guard against heart disease and cancer. This is because of the antioxidant nutrients found in walnuts: selenium, zinc, copper and vitamin E.

Each tartlet provides

kcal 145, **protein** 4 g, **fat** 7 g (of which saturated fat 2 g), **carbohydrate** 19 g (of which sugars 3 g), **fibre** 1 g

✓✓	E
✓	B₁, copper, selenium

Smoked turkey and apricot bites

Dried apricots moistened with orange juice, then wrapped in smoked turkey rashers make a tasty snack to pass round with drinks, as well as an interesting garnish for a festive roast chicken or turkey. Take care when grilling turkey rashers – they cook more quickly than bacon and, because they contain no fat, will dry out if overcooked.

Makes 24 bites

24 ready-to-eat dried apricots

juice of 1 orange

2 tsp marmalade

2 tsp wholegrain mustard

6 smoked turkey rashers, about 150 g
    (5½ oz) in total

1 tsp extra virgin olive oil

chopped fresh flat-leaf parsley to garnish
    (optional)

Preparation time: 10 minutes

Cooking time: 2 minutes

1 Place the apricots in a small bowl, sprinkle over the orange juice and toss so that they are moistened all over (this will prevent them from burning under the grill).

2 Mix the marmalade with the mustard. Spread each turkey rasher with a little of the mustard mixture, then, using scissors, cut it in half lengthways. Cut each piece in half again, this time across the middle, to make a total of 24 strips of turkey.

3 Preheat the grill to moderate. Drain the apricots. Wrap a strip of turkey around each apricot and secure it with a wooden cocktail stick.

4 Arrange the turkey bites on the grill pan, then brush each with a little oil. Grill for 1 minute on each side or until the turkey is just cooked.

5 Pile the bites in a small shallow bowl and sprinkle with chopped parsley, if using. Serve hot.

Some more ideas

● Instead of the mustard and marmalade mixture, spread the turkey rashers with a little pesto sauce.

● Cherry tomatoes can be used instead of dried apricots. They do not need to be moistened with orange juice.

● To make smoked turkey and banana chutney bites, cut 3 medium-sized bananas into chunky

pieces (8 pieces each) and toss in a little lemon or lime juice to prevent them from discolouring. Wrap each piece in a strip of turkey rasher that has been spread with a little mango chutney, then grill for 1 minute on each side. Serve hot.

● For fresh pineapple and Black Forest bites, peel a small pineapple, about 900 g (2 lb) with the leaves. Cut into quarters lengthways and trim away the woody core. Cut each quarter across into 8 to make 32 wedge-shaped pieces in total. Cut 8 slices of Black Forest ham in half lengthways, then cut each piece across in half. Wrap a strip of ham around each wedge of pineapple and secure with a wooden cocktail stick. Serve as soon as possible.

Plus points

● Ready-to-eat dried apricots are a useful item to have on hand for healthy meals. They are one of the richest fruit sources of iron and a useful source of calcium.

● Turkey rashers offer an excellent lower-fat alternative to bacon: 100 g (3½ oz) contains 1.6 g fat and 99 kcals, whereas the same weight of back bacon contains 21 g fat and 249 kcals.

Fish dim sum

These steamed dumplings made with wonton wrappers look especially appealing served in Chinese bamboo steamers. Provide your guests with cocktail sticks to help with dipping the dim sum and eating them.

Makes 28 dim sum

1 tbsp sunflower oil

1 carrot, finely diced

1 tbsp finely chopped fresh root ginger

1 garlic clove, crushed

4 spring onions, chopped

½ tsp toasted sesame oil

100 g (3½ oz) baby spinach leaves, finely shredded

280 g (10 oz) piece of skinless cod fillet

1 egg white

2 tbsp cornflour

28 wonton wrappers

salt

To garnish

1 carrot

2 spring onions, finely shredded

To serve

4 tbsp dry sherry

4 tbsp soy sauce

Preparation time: 40 minutes
Cooking time: 10 minutes

Each dim sum provides

kcal 36, **protein** 2.5 g, **fat** 1 g (of which saturated fat 0.1 g), **carbohydrate** 3 g (of which sugars 1 g), **fibre** 0.5 g

✓ A, E

1 Heat the sunflower oil in a small saucepan. Add the carrot, ginger, garlic and spring onions, and cook, stirring occasionally, for 5 minutes or until the carrot is slightly softened. Stir in the sesame oil and spinach, and cook for a few more seconds or until the spinach has wilted. Increase the heat to high and cook for about 30 seconds to evaporate excess liquid, then remove from the heat. Set aside to cool slightly.

2 Purée the cod fillet in a food processor. Alternatively, finely chop the fish, then pound it with the back of a wooden spoon until it binds together. Lightly whisk the egg white with the cornflour in a large mixing bowl. Mix in the fish, then add the carrot and spinach mixture with salt to taste. Stir until all the ingredients are combined in a fairly stiff paste. Set aside.

3 To prepare the garnish, cut 28 thin slices from the carrot. Lay them over the bottom of 2 bamboo steaming baskets, setting the slices slightly apart. Finely shred the remaining carrot.

4 To fill the dim sum, lay a wonton wrapper on the palm of one hand. Use a teaspoon to place a little fish mixture on the middle of the wrapper. Dampen the edges with a little water and bring up the sides of the wrapper around the filling. Pinch the edges together at the top to seal.

5 Gently tap the base of the dim sum on the work surface so that it stands up with straight sides, then set it on a slice of carrot in one of the steamers. Repeat with the remaining wrappers and filling. (The dim sum can be prepared up to 6 hours ahead and kept in the fridge, covered with cling film.)

6 Steam over boiling water for 10 minutes. If you do not have stacking bamboo steaming baskets, cook the dim sum in 2 batches. When the first batch is done, transfer it to a heatproof plate, cover loosely with foil and keep hot over a pan of simmering water while cooking the second batch.

7 While the dim sum are cooking, mix together the sherry and soy sauce in a small bowl. Garnish the hot dim sum with the shredded carrot and spring onion, and serve with the soy and sherry dipping sauce.

Plus point

● White fish such as cod is low in calories and an excellent source of iodine. Fish is one of the most reliable sources of this important mineral because the iodine content of sea water is much more consistent than the iodine content of soil.

special bites

Some more ideas

• Chinese pancakes can be used instead of wonton wrappers. Cut each pancake into 3 wedges. Place a little filling on a wedge and roll up into a cornet shape. Cut thin strips of carrot instead of circles and use these as a base for cooking the dim sum as in the main recipe.

• To make mushroom and tofu dim sum, soak 4 dried shiitake mushrooms in a little boiling water for 10 minutes to rehydrate, then drain, squeezing out excess water. Discard the tough stalks and chop the mushroom caps. Cook the shiitake with 100 g (3½ oz) chopped button or chestnut mushrooms, 1 finely diced carrot, 1 crushed garlic clove, 1 tbsp finely chopped fresh root ginger and 4 chopped spring onions for 5 minutes, then increase the heat and cook rapidly, stirring, until all the liquid from the mushrooms has evaporated. Mash 300 g (10½ oz) firm tofu with a fork. Mix in 4 tbsp cornflour, then add the vegetables and 1 tbsp chopped fresh coriander. Use to fill the wonton wrappers and steam as in the main recipe.

Stuffed mushrooms

Filled with a delicious combination of finely chopped courgette, spinach and hazelnuts, then topped with grated Parmesan cheese and baked, these mushrooms make a very tasty, hard-to-resist party bite. They look their best if the mushrooms used are all about the same size.

Makes 16 mushrooms

16 large closed-cap chestnut mushrooms or
   small field mushrooms, all about 4 cm
   (1½ in) diameter, about 250 g (8½ oz)
   in total
30 g (1 oz) butter
2 shallots, finely chopped
1 garlic clove, crushed
1 small courgette, finely chopped
15 g (½ oz) baby spinach leaves, finely
   shredded, plus extra leaves to garnish
   (optional)
30 g (1 oz) fresh wholemeal breadcrumbs
30 g (1 oz) hazelnuts, finely chopped
2 tbsp finely chopped parsley
45 g (1½ oz) Parmesan cheese, freshly grated
salt and pepper

Preparation time: 25–30 minutes
Cooking time: 15 minutes

1 Preheat the oven to 180°C (350°F, gas mark 4). Remove the stalks from the mushrooms and chop them finely. Melt the butter in a frying pan, add the chopped mushroom stalks, shallots, garlic and courgette, and cook for 5 minutes, stirring occasionally.

2 Remove the pan from the heat and stir in the shredded spinach, breadcrumbs, hazelnuts, parsley, and salt and pepper to taste.

3 Put the mushroom caps, hollow side up, in a single layer in a lightly greased shallow ovenproof dish or on a lightly greased baking tray. Heap some of the shallot and courgette mixture into each mushroom cap and sprinkle the Parmesan cheese over the top. (The mushrooms can be prepared 2–3 hours ahead and kept, covered with cling film, in the fridge.)

4 Bake for about 15 minutes or until the mushrooms are tender and the cheese has melted. Serve warm, on a bed of spinach leaves, if liked.

Some more ideas

• For mushrooms stuffed with spring greens and walnuts, use spring greens in place of the spinach, 1 small red onion in place of the shallots, chopped walnuts in place of the hazelnuts, and fresh basil or coriander in place of the parsley.

• Make mushrooms with red pepper and pine nut filling. Sauté the mushroom stalks in 1 tbsp extra virgin olive oil with 4 finely chopped spring onions, ½ small seeded and finely chopped red pepper and 1 crushed garlic clove for 5 minutes. Stir in 30 g (1 oz) chopped pine nuts, 15 g (½ oz) chopped watercress, 30 g (1 oz) fresh breadcrumbs, 2 tbsp finely chopped parsley, and salt and pepper to taste. Fill the mushroom caps with this mixture and sprinkle with 45 g (1½ oz) finely grated mozzarella cheese. Bake as in the main recipe.

Plus points

• Mushrooms provide useful amounts of some of the B vitamins and are a good source of the trace mineral copper. This mineral has several functions – it is found in many enzymes, and is needed for bone growth as well as for the formation of connective tissue.

• Hazelnuts were known in China 5000 years ago and were also eaten by the Romans. They are a particularly good source of vitamin E and most of the B vitamins (with the exception of vitamin B_{12}).

Each mushroom provides
kcal 46, **protein** 2 g, **fat** 4 g (of which saturated fat 2 g), **carbohydrate** 1 g (of which sugars 0.5 g), **fibre** 0.5 g

✓ E, selenium

special bites

Pissaladière

Pissaladière is a Provençal relative of Italian pizza. The thick bread base, enriched with olive oil, is topped with a flavoursome tomato and onion mixture, then decorated with a lattice of anchovies and black olives. Serve warm or cool, cut in bite-sized squares for canapés, or into 16 larger snack-sized squares.

Makes 64 bite-sized squares

Dough
450 g (1 lb) strong (bread) flour, plus extra for kneading

1 tsp salt

1 sachet easy-blend dried yeast, about 7 g

3 tbsp extra virgin olive oil

300 ml (10 fl oz) hand-hot water

Topping
3 tbsp extra virgin olive oil

4 onions, about 750 g (1 lb 10 oz) in total, thinly sliced

2 garlic cloves, crushed

1 can chopped tomatoes in rich tomato juice, about 400 g

2 tbsp tomato purée

1 tbsp chopped fresh oregano

2 cans anchovy fillets, about 50 g each, drained and halved lengthways

16 stoned black olives, about 55 g (2 oz) in total, quartered

pepper

Preparation time: 1½ hours, plus 1 hour rising
Cooking time: 40 minutes

Each square provides
kcal 44, **protein** 1.5 g, **fat** 1.5 g (of which saturated fat 0.2 g), **carbohydrate** 6.5 g (of which sugars 1 g), **fibre** 0.5 g

1 For the dough, sift the flour and salt into a bowl, then stir in the yeast. Make a well in the centre and pour in the oil and water. Gradually mix the dry ingredients into the liquids, using a spoon at first and then your hand, to make a soft, slightly sticky dough.

2 Turn the dough out onto a lightly floured surface and knead for 10 minutes or until the dough is smooth and springy. Place in a lightly oiled bowl, cover with cling film and leave in a warm place to rise for about 45 minutes or until doubled in size.

3 Meanwhile, make the topping. Heat the oil in a large saucepan, add the onions and garlic, and cook over a low heat for about 40 minutes or until very soft and lightly golden but not browned. Add the tomatoes with their juice, the tomato purée, oregano and pepper to taste, and cook gently for a further 10 minutes, stirring ocasionally. Remove from the heat and leave to cool.

4 When the dough has risen, knock it back and knead again gently. Roll it out on a floured surface to a 30 cm (12 in) square and place on a lightly oiled baking sheet.

5 Preheat the oven to 200°C (400°F, gas mark 6). Spread the onion mixture evenly over the dough square, then make a criss-cross pattern on top with the anchovy fillets. Place the olive quarters in the squares. Leave the pissaladière to rise at room temperature for about 15 minutes.

6 Bake the pissaladière for about 30 minutes or until the crust is golden and firm, then reduce the oven temperature to 190°C (375°F, gas mark 5) and bake for a further 10 minutes. Allow to cool slightly before cutting into squares for serving.

Plus points
• This pissaladière is made with a thick bread base, providing generous starchy carbohydrate. As white flour by law must contain added iron, calcium, vitamin B$_1$ and niacin, the bread base can also make a contribution to the intake of these nutrients.

• Canned tomatoes are a nutritious storecupboard ingredient as the canning process does not destroy the lycopene content but rather enhances it. Lycopene is a phytochemical with powerful antioxidant properties.

Some more ideas

- For an onion and pancetta pissaladière, leave the tomatoes and tomato purée out of the onion mixture. Cut 100 g (3½ oz) thin slices of smoked pancetta in half lengthways, twist them and lay them on top of the onion mixture in a criss-cross pattern. Place whole capers in the squares in between.

- Make a tomato and red pepper pissaladière. Cover the dough base with a thin layer of passata, then arrange a mixture of sliced fresh tomatoes, strips of sun-dried tomatoes and coarsely chopped, grilled and peeled red peppers over the top. Brush with a little extra virgin olive oil, sprinkle over some freshly ground black pepper and bake as in the main recipe. Serve garnished with fresh basil leaves scattered over the top.

Chicken yakitori

These delicious Japanese-style bites of chicken speared with green pepper and spring onions can be assembled in advance and then grilled just before serving. For the best flavour, leave the chicken to marinate for several hours or overnight, and remember to soak the skewers first so they do not burn under the grill.

Makes 30 kebabs

3 tbsp shoyu (Japanese soy sauce)

3 tbsp sake or dry sherry

1 tbsp toasted sesame oil

1 garlic clove, crushed

1 tbsp finely chopped fresh root ginger

2 tsp clear honey

500 g (1 lb 2 oz) skinless boneless chicken
   breasts (fillets), cut into 2 cm (¾ in) cubes

1 large green pepper, seeded and cut into
   30 small cubes

4 large spring onions, cut across into
   30 pieces

Preparation time: 20 minutes, plus at least
   1 hour marinating

Cooking time: 10–15 minutes

1 Place the shoyu, sake or sherry, sesame oil, garlic, ginger and honey in a shallow dish and stir together to mix. Add the chicken pieces and spoon the marinade over them. Cover and marinate in the fridge for at least 1 hour or overnight.

2 Just before cooking, put 30 short wooden skewers in warm water and leave to soak for 10 minutes. Preheat the grill to moderate.

3 Thread about 2 pieces of chicken onto each skewer, alternating with a piece of pepper and one of spring onion, threaded widthways. Place the kebabs on the grill pan and cook under the grill for 10–15 minutes or until tender, turning from time to time and brushing with the marinade. Serve hot.

Some more ideas

• Sprinkle the kebabs with a few sesame seeds towards the end of the grilling time.

• An alternative marinade is 3 tbsp hoisin sauce mixed with 2 tbsp Chinese rice wine or dry sherry and 1 tbsp groundnut oil. If liked, add ½ tsp five-spice powder or ½ finely chopped and seeded fresh red chilli.

• Instead of green pepper, use pieces of baby leeks, red or orange peppers, courgette or tiny mushroom caps.

• For salmon yakitori, use 500 g (1 lb 2 oz) skinless salmon fillet and marinate in a mixture of 3 tbsp shoyu or other soy sauce, 2 tbsp dry sherry, 1 tbsp groundnut oil, 1 crushed garlic clove, 1 tsp clear honey and the grated zest of 1 small orange for about 30 minutes. Thread onto soaked wooden skewers, alternating the cubes of salmon with whole firm cherry tomatoes and pieces of spring onion. Grill for 10–15 minutes, turning and basting frequently with the marinade.

Each kebab provides

kcal 25, protein 4 g, fat 0.5 g (of which saturated fat 0.1 g), carbohydrate 1 g (of which sugars 0.5 g), fibre 0.1 g

✓   C, niacin

Plus points

• Many party food nibbles are made with pastry and are high in fat and calories. These little kebabs, made with lean chicken and vegetables, offer a lower-fat choice and look really appealing.

• Honey has been used since ancient times as a sweetener and preservative. It has a higher fructose content than sugar, which makes it sweeter and it is also lower in calories on a weight for weight basis because of its higher water content.

Goat's cheese toasts

Indulge your guests with these tasty morsels, made by topping toasted slices of crusty baguette with slices of plum tomato and tangy goat's cheese, sprinkled with pine nuts and fresh herbs. Choose your favourite type of goat's cheese: delicate or strong in flavour, soft or firm in texture.

Makes 16 toasts

1 baguette, about 280 g (10 oz), cut into
    2.5 cm (1 in) slices
4 tbsp passata
2 tbsp sun-dried tomato paste
4 plum tomatoes, about 250 g (8½ oz) in total
140 g (5 oz) goat's cheese
1½ tbsp extra virgin olive oil
15 g (½ oz) pine nuts
few sprigs of fresh thyme or oregano, plus
    extra to garnish

Preparation time: 15 minutes
Cooking time: 4–5 minutes

Each toast provides ⓥ
kcal 89, **protein** 3 g, **fat** 4 g (of which
saturated fat 1 g), **carbohydrate** 11 g (of
which sugars 1 g), **fibre** 0.5 g

✓   E

1 Preheat the grill to moderate. Place the baguette slices on a rack in the grill pan and lightly toast on both sides.

2 Mix together the passata and tomato paste and spread a little on top of each toast, covering the surface completely.

3 Slice the tomatoes lengthways, discarding a slim slice from the curved edges, to give 4 flat slices from each tomato. Lay a slice of tomato on top of each toast.

4 Place 1 small slice of firm goat's cheese or about 1 tsp of soft goat's cheese on top of each tomato slice, and drizzle over a little olive oil. Scatter on a few pine nuts and thyme or oregano leaves.

5 Grill for 4–5 minutes or until the cheese is beginning to melt and the pine nuts are golden. Serve the toasts hot, garnished with sprigs of thyme or oregano.

Some more ideas
• Use a goat's cheese flavoured with garlic and herbs.
• Serve the toasts on a bed of mixed soft salad leaves as a starter or light lunch. Allow 4 toasts per serving.
• Make fruity goat's cheese toasts. Instead of the tomato topping, mix together 2 tbsp each of cranberry sauce and mango, peach or another fruit chutney. Spread this over the toasts, top with the goat's cheese and scatter over a few flaked almonds, then grill as in the main recipe.
• For tapenade goat's cheese toasts, put 100 g (3½ oz) stoned black olives, 1 can anchovy fillets, about 50 g, drained, 3 tbsp drained capers, 3 tbsp extra virgin olive oil, the juice of ½ lemon and 2 crushed garlic cloves in a blender or food processor and blend to a paste (or pound to a paste with a pestle and mortar). This makes 220 g (scant 8 oz) tapenade; it can be kept, covered, in the fridge for 2 weeks. Spread onto 4 large, thick slices of toasted bread, then top with the goat's cheese and grill for 3–4 minutes. Cut each slice into 8 fingers or triangles and serve warm, sprinkled with chopped parsley. Makes 32 toasts.

Plus points
• Pine nuts, used in Middle Eastern rice dishes and stuffings and an important ingredient in Italian pesto sauce, are rich in a variety of minerals including magnesium, potassium, iron, zinc and copper.
• Goat's cheese is a tasty source of protein and calcium, as well as B vitamins (B_1, B_6, B_{12} and niacin) and phosphorus. A medium-fat goat's cheese contains about half the fat of Cheddar cheese.

special bites

129

Sushi rolls

Japanese food tends to be low in fat, and these stylish sushi rolls are no exception. Now that the ingredients are available in supermarkets, it is easy to make them yourself. You must use sushi rice, which is sticky when cooked.

Makes 32 sushi rolls

300 g (10½ oz) sushi rice

2 tbsp caster sugar

1 tsp salt

3 tbsp rice wine vinegar

2 spring onions, very finely chopped

30 g (1 oz) piece of cucumber, seeded and finely chopped

115 g (4 oz) smoked salmon

4 sheets of sushi nori, about 10 g (scant ½ oz) in total

2 tsp wasabi paste

To serve (optional)

gari (pickled ginger)

shoyu or tamari (Japanese soy sauce)

Preparation and cooking time: 35 minutes, plus cooling

Each sushi roll provides

kcal 45, protein 2 g, fat 0.4 g (of which saturated fat 0.1 g), carbohydrate 8 g (of which sugars 1 g), fibre 0.2 g

1 Cook the sushi rice in a saucepan of boiling water according to the packet instructions.

2 Meanwhile, put the sugar, salt and vinegar in a small saucepan and heat gently until the sugar dissolves. When the rice is cooked, drizzle the mixture over it, then add the spring onions and cucumber, and mix. Cover with a tea-towel and leave to cool.

3 Divide the sushi rice into 4 equal portions. Cut the salmon into strips about 1 cm (½ in) wide. Place a sheet of nori, shiny side down, on a bamboo mat, or on a sheet of baking parchment on a board. Spread a portion of rice over the nori, pressing it down evenly and leaving a 1 cm (½ in) space at the top and bottom. Place one-quarter of the salmon along the middle of the layer of rice, then spread the salmon with ½ tsp of the wasabi paste.

4 With the help of the bamboo mat or parchment, roll up the nori and rice into a neat tube. Roll tightly to ensure that the rice sticks together and holds the filling in place. Make 3 more rolls in the same way.

5 Using a wet knife, cut each roll across into 8 slices and stand them upright on a serving plate. Rinse the knife between cuts. If liked, garnish with pieces of gari and offer a small dish of shoyu or tamari for dipping.

Some more ideas

• For prawn sushi, chop 115 g (4 oz) cooked peeled prawns and stir into the cooled rice in place of smoked salmon. Omit the wasabi.

• To make mushroom and carrot sushi, put 4 large dried shiitake mushrooms in a small saucepan, cover with cold water and leave to soak for 30 minutes. Lift out the mushrooms and remove their stalks. Return the mushroom caps to the soaking liquid in the pan, together with 1 small carrot, cut into matchstick strips. Simmer for 4–5 minutes or until tender; drain. Thinly slice the mushrooms. Cut ½ cucumber into quarters lengthways and remove the seeds, then cut into very thin strips the same length as a nori sheet. Spread each sheet of nori with sushi rice, then place a line of cooked mushrooms and carrot down the middle and top with a few strips of cucumber. Roll up and slice as in the main recipe. Sprinkle 2 tbsp black or toasted white sesame seeds on a plate and dip in the ends of the sushi rolls to coat lightly.

Plus point

• Like other foods from the sea, nori – a dark brownish seaweed – is a good source of iodine, essential for the healthy functioning of the thyroid gland. It also provides excellent amounts of calcium, potassium and vitamin A.

Greek meatballs with lemon dip

These little meatballs, made from a mixture of minced lamb and rice, flavoured with thyme, lemon and nutmeg, are grilled on sticks for easy eating. The classic Greek egg and lemon dipping sauce served alongside has a tangy flavour, which is a perfect complement for the meatballs.

Makes 24 kebabs

30 g (1 oz) long-grain rice
2 small red onions
400 g (14 oz) lean minced lamb
1 small onion, very finely chopped
1 garlic clove, crushed
1 tbsp chopped fresh thyme
½ tsp freshly grated nutmeg
finely grated zest of 1 lemon
1 large red pepper, seeded and cut into
    24 small squares
extra virgin olive oil for brushing
salt and pepper

Egg and lemon dip

1½ tsp arrowroot
juice of 2 small lemons
100 ml (3½ fl oz) lamb or chicken stock
1 small egg
2 tsp chopped fresh thyme
salt and pepper

Preparation time: 25 minutes
Cooking time: 20–25 minutes

Each kebab provides

kcal 36, **protein** 4 g, **fat** 1.5 g (of which saturated fat 0.1 g), **carbohydrate** 2 g (of which sugars 1 g), **fibre** 0.2 g

✓   A, C

1 Place the rice in a pan, cover with cold water and bring to the boil. Cook for 10 minutes or according to the packet instructions. Drain and set aside.

2 Soak 24 long wooden cocktail sticks in warm water for about 10 minutes, then drain. Preheat the grill to moderate.

3 Cut each red onion into 12 thin wedges, keeping them still attached at the root end.

4 Combine the minced lamb, finely chopped onion, cooked rice, garlic, thyme, nutmeg and lemon zest in a bowl, and season with salt and pepper to taste. Mix well together using your hands. Shape the meat mixture into 24 small balls.

5 Thread a meatball, 1 piece of pepper and 1 onion wedge onto each cocktail stick. Arrange in one layer on a rack in the grill pan. (The kebabs can be prepared 3–4 hours ahead and then kept in the fridge, covered with cling film.) Brush lightly with oil and grill for 15–18 minutes, turning occasionally, until golden brown and thoroughly cooked.

6 Meanwhile, make the dip. Mix the arrowroot with about half of the lemon juice, then stir in the rest. Heat the stock in a small saucepan until boiling, then stir in the arrowroot and

lemon juice mixture. Bring back to the boil, stirring constantly, then remove from the heat.

7 Put the egg in a bowl and whisk lightly. Slowly pour in the hot stock mixture in a thin, steady stream, whisking constantly. Return to the pan and whisk over a low heat for about 4 minutes or until the sauce is smooth and thick. Do not boil or the egg may curdle and spoil the texture. Stir in the chopped thyme, and season with salt and pepper to taste.

8 Serve the meatball skewers with the hot lemon sauce.

Plus points

• Minced lamb can have quite a high fat content, but because these meatballs are grilled, much of the excess fat is drained off.
• Making the meatballs with a mixture of lamb and rice means less meat is used than normal, and healthy starchy carbohydrates are added with the rice.

special bites

132

Some more ideas

- Instead of red pepper, use green or yellow, or replace the pepper with wedges of bulb fennel.
- For a quick and easy lemon-mint dip that needs no cooking, stir the finely grated zest of 1 lemon and 2 tbsp chopped fresh mint into 200 g (7 oz) Greek-style yogurt.
- To make turkey and sage meatballs, replace the minced lamb with minced turkey, and use 55 g (2 oz) fresh white, Granary or wholemeal breadcrumbs instead of the rice. Flavour the turkey mixture with 1 tbsp chopped fresh sage in place of thyme. Make the lemon dip with chicken or turkey stock, and chopped sage instead of thyme.

Sesame cheese twists

These crisp cheese sticks are delicious served fresh and still warm from the oven. Enriched with egg yolks and well-flavoured with freshly grated Parmesan cheese, they are made with a combination of wholemeal and plain flour, so that they are substantial without being at all heavy.

Makes 40 sticks

85 g (3 oz) plain wholemeal flour, preferably stoneground

85 g (3 oz) plain white flour, plus extra for rolling

¼ tsp salt

45 g (1½ oz) butter

45 g (1½ oz) Parmesan cheese, freshly grated

1 large egg

2 tbsp semi-skimmed milk

1 tsp paprika

1 tbsp sesame seeds

Preparation time: 10–15 minutes

Cooking time: 15 minutes

Each stick provides Ⓥ

kcal 32, **protein** 1 g, **fat** 2 g (of which saturated fat 1 g), **carbohydrate** 3 g (of which sugars 0.1 g), **fibre** 0.3 g

1 Preheat the oven to 180ºC (350ºF, gas mark 4). Sift the flours and salt into a bowl, tipping in the bran left in the sieve. Rub in the butter until the mixture resembles fine breadcrumbs. Stir in the Parmesan cheese.

2 Whisk the egg and milk together. Reserve 1 tsp of this mixture, and stir the rest into the dry ingredients to make a firm dough. Knead on a lightly floured surface for a few seconds or until smooth.

3 Sprinkle the paprika over the floured surface, then roll out the dough on it to form a square slightly larger than 20 cm (8 in). Trim the edges to make them straight. Brush the dough with the reserved egg mixture and sprinkle over the sesame seeds. Cut the square of dough in half, then cut into 10 cm (4 in) sticks that are about 1 cm (½ in) wide.

4 Twist the sticks and place on a large baking sheet lined with baking parchment. Lightly press the ends of the sticks down so that they do not untwist during baking.

5 Bake for 15 minutes or until lightly browned and crisp. Cool on the baking sheets for a few minutes, then serve warm, or transfer to a wire rack to cool completely. The sticks can be kept in an airtight tin for up to 5 days.

Some more ideas

• Use finely grated mature Cheddar cheese instead of the Parmesan.

• For blue cheese and walnut biscuits, mash 30 g (1 oz) blue cheese, such as Gorgonzola, Stilton or Danish blue, with 55 g (2 oz) softened butter. Sift over 45 g (1½ oz) plain wholemeal flour, 30 g (1 oz) self-raising white flour and 30 g (1 oz) ground rice, tipping in the bran left in the sieve. Add 30 g (1 oz) chopped toasted walnuts. Rub together, then knead lightly to form a dough. Shape into a roll about 12 cm (5 in) long. Wrap in cling film and chill for about 30 minutes. Cut into thin slices, arrange on a baking sheet lined with baking parchment and bake in a preheated 190ºC (375ºF, gas mark 5) oven for 15 minutes. Transfer to a wire rack to cool. Makes about 16 biscuits.

Plus points

• Sesame seeds are a good source of calcium as well as providing iron and zinc.

• Wholemeal flour has a lot to offer: dietary fibre, B vitamins and vitamin E, together with iron, selenium and magnesium. Stoneground wholemeal flour has slightly more B vitamins than factory-milled wholemeal flour, because stonegrinding keeps the grain cool. Milling with metal rollers creates heat, which spoils some of the nutrients.

Sweet Treats

A little of what you fancy . . .

WHEN YOU WANT SOMETHING SWEET, don't just reach for a biscuit or a chocolate bar! Instead, why not enjoy a home-made treat that is just as satisfying and that will make a nutritious contribution to your diet? Drop scones, full of fruit and nuts, are delicious warm from the pan, drizzled with maple syrup. American-style blueberry and raspberry muffins are delightful warm or cool, or you might fancy crumpets with a spicy banana cream topping. Flapjacks, a sticky teabread and 'slice and bake' biscuits can be made ahead and kept in a tin, for instant access or packing in a lunchbox. Or you could whiz up a smoothie from fresh fruit, milk and yogurt.

Orange and pecan biscuits

These are 'slice-and-bake' biscuits – the roll of dough can be prepared in advance and kept in the fridge. Then, whenever biscuits are wanted, you simply slice the roll into rounds, top with pecan nuts and bake.

Makes 24 biscuits

55 g (2 oz) plain wholemeal flour, plus extra
    for kneading
55 g (2 oz) self-raising white flour
85 g (3 oz) light muscovado sugar
55 g (2 oz) ground rice
30 g (1 oz) pecan nuts, chopped
grated zest of 1 orange
4 tbsp sunflower oil
1 large egg
24 pecan nut halves to decorate

Preparation time: 15 minutes, plus 2 hours
    chilling
Cooking time: 8–10 minutes

1 Put the wholemeal and self-raising flours, sugar, ground rice, chopped pecan nuts and orange zest in a bowl, and stir until well combined.

2 In a small bowl, beat the oil and egg together with a fork. Add this mixture to the dry ingredients and mix with a fork until they come together to make a dough.

3 Knead the dough very lightly on a floured surface until smooth, then roll into a sausage shape about 30 cm (12 in) long. Wrap in cling film and chill for 2 hours. (The dough can be kept in the fridge for 2–3 days before slicing and baking.)

4 Preheat the oven to 180°C (350°F, gas mark 4). Unwrap the roll of dough and lightly reshape to a neat sausage, if necessary.

5 Cut the roll across into 24 slices using a sharp knife. Arrange the slices, spaced apart, on 2 large non-stick baking sheets. Top each slice with a pecan nut half, pressing it in slightly.

6 Bake for about 10 minutes or until firm to the touch and lightly golden. Transfer the biscuits to a wire rack to cool completely. They can be stored in an airtight tin for up to 5 days.

Some more ideas

● Instead of the sunflower oil, use 55 g (2 oz) melted butter.

● Chopped hazelnuts can be used in place of the pecans, with whole hazelnuts to decorate.

● To make almond polenta biscuits, mix 55 g (2 oz) instant polenta with 85 g (3 oz) icing sugar and 115 g (4 oz) self-raising flour. Rub in 55 g (2 oz) butter until the mixture resembles breadcrumbs. Beat 1 large egg with ½ tsp pure almond extract, add to the crumb mixture and mix to form a soft dough. Roll, wrap and chill as in the main recipe. Before baking, scatter 30 g (1 oz) flaked almonds over the slices.

Plus points

● Like other nuts, pecans are rich in fat – up to 70 g per 100 g (3½ oz) – but little of this is saturated fat, the majority being present as polyunsaturated fat. Pecans also provide generous amounts of vitamin E.

● Sunflower oil is one of the most widely used vegetable oils because of its mild flavour, and it works well in biscuits and other baked goods in place of saturated fats such as butter. It is a particularly good source of vitamin E, a powerful antioxidant. Polyunsaturated fats, such as are found in sunflower oil, are more susceptible to rancidity than saturated fats, but the vitamin E content helps to stop the oil going rancid.

Each biscuit provides

kcal 106, **protein** 2 g, **fat** 7 g (of which saturated fat 1 g), **carbohydrate** 9 g (of which sugars 4 g), **fibre** 1 g

✓✓	E
✓	copper

Caramelised banana crumpets

Forget about smothering toasted crumpets in butter; this low-fat topping is really yummy and much healthier. Lightly mashed bananas are mixed with creamy fromage frais and warm spices and piled onto crumpet fingers, then finished by drizzling with honey and grilled until bubbling. It's the perfect quick sweet snack.

Serves 4

8 crumpet fingers, about 30 g (1 oz) each
2 medium-sized bananas
4 tbsp fromage frais
seeds from 4 cardamom pods, crushed
½ tsp ground cinnamon, plus extra to sprinkle
1 tsp finely grated orange zest
8 tsp clear honey

Preparation and cooking time: 15 minutes

1 Preheat the grill to high. Arrange the crumpet fingers on the rack of the grill pan and toast for 2–3 minutes on each side or until browned and crisp.

2 Meanwhile, mash the bananas with a fork, keeping them a bit textured. Add the fromage frais, cardamom seeds, cinnamon and orange zest, and mix well together.

3 Spread the banana mixture over the tops of the toasted crumpets, levelling the surface, then drizzle each with 1 tsp of the honey.

4 Return to the grill and cook for 2–3 minutes or until the tops are lightly browned and the honey is bubbling. Leave the crumpets to cool slightly, then sprinkle over a little extra cinnamon and serve.

Some more ideas

● Use wholemeal crumpets for added fibre. If you cannot find crumpet fingers, you can simply cut square crumpets in half.

● Instead of cardamom seeds, use ¼–½ tsp ground cardamom or freshly grated nutmeg, to taste.

● For nectarine or peach brioche fingers, cut 4 thick slices, about 20 g (¾ oz) each, from a brioche loaf. Toast under a preheated grill for about 30 seconds on each side. Divide 115 g (4 oz) ricotta cheese among the toasts and spread over one side, right to the edges (any exposed bread will burn). Cut each slice of brioche in half. Scatter over 45 g (1½ oz) toasted flaked almonds. Thinly slice 1 large ripe nectarine or peach and arrange on top, covering the almonds to prevent them from getting too brown. Drizzle each finger with 1 tsp maple syrup and grill for 3–4 minutes or until golden and sizzling. Leave the brioche fingers to cool slightly before serving.

Plus points

● Bananas are a concentrated source of energy and one of the best fruit sources of the mineral potassium, which is vital for muscle and nerve functions. This is why bananas are very popular with sportsmen and women.

● Fromage frais, a soft cheese originating in France, is lower in fat than most other creamy cheeses. It is available in varying fat contents, from 8% down to 0%. Whichever version you choose, fromage frais can make a good contribution to calcium intake.

Each serving provides

kcal 262, protein 7 g, fat 4 g (of which saturated fat 2 g), carbohydrate 53 g (of which sugars 29 g), fibre 2 g

✓ B₂, B₆, B₁₂, C, niacin, calcium

sweet treats

Apple and hazelnut drop scones

Drop scones are an almost instant sweet snack. The thick batter is made by simply stirring together a few basic storecupboard ingredients, and the scones cook in minutes. Here they are flavoured with diced apple and toasted hazelnuts. Top with a little maple syrup and enjoy warm from the pan.

Makes 16 scones

45 g (1½ oz) skinned hazelnuts, chopped
200 g (7 oz) plain flour
½ tsp bicarbonate of soda
pinch of salt
2 tbsp caster sugar
1 large egg
250 ml (8½ fl oz) buttermilk
1 dessert apple, about 150 g (5½ oz), cored
   and finely chopped
1 tbsp sunflower oil
4 tbsp maple syrup

Preparation time: 15 minutes
Cooking time: 20 minutes

Each scone provides Ⓥ

kcal 106, protein 3 g, fat 3 g (of which
saturated fat 0.5 g), carbohydrate 18 g (of
which sugars 8 g), fibre 1 g

✓✓   E

1 Heat a small non-stick frying pan, add the hazelnuts and cook until golden brown, stirring and tossing constantly. Take care not to overcook the nuts as they burn easily. Tip them into a small bowl.

2 Sift the flour, bicarbonate of soda, salt and sugar into a large mixing bowl. Make a well in the centre. Lightly beat the egg with the buttermilk and pour into the well. Gradually whisk the flour mixture into the buttermilk mixture to make a smooth, thick batter. Add the apple and toasted hazelnuts, and stir in with a large metal spoon.

3 Lightly brush a griddle or heavy frying pan with a little of the sunflower oil, then heat over a moderate heat. Depending on the size of the griddle or pan, you can cook about 4 scones at the same time. For each one, drop a heaped tablespoon of batter onto the hot surface. Bubbles will rise to the surface and burst. Gently slip a small palette knife under the drop scone to loosen it, then cook for a further minute or until the underside is golden brown. Turn the scone over and cook the other side for 1–2 minutes or until golden.

4 Remove the scones from the griddle or frying pan and keep warm under a clean cloth. Cook the rest of the batter in the same way.

5 When all the drop scones are cooked, quickly heat the maple syrup in a small saucepan just to warm it. Drizzle the syrup over the warm drop scones and serve immediately.

Some more ideas

• For apricot and walnut or pecan drop scones, use 75 g (2½ oz) chopped ready-to-eat dried apricots instead of the apple, and 45 g (1½ oz) walnuts or pecans instead of the hazelnuts.

• Make fresh berry drop scones by adding 100 g (3½ oz) blackberries or raspberries to the batter in place of the apple, and seasoning with a good pinch of ground mixed spice. Omit the hazelnuts, if you prefer.

Plus points

• Buttermilk is the liquid left over after cream has been turned into butter by churning. Contrary to its name, buttermilk does not contain butterfat, but it does provides protein, minerals and milk sugar or lactose, as well as a delightfully piquant taste.

• Apples are a good source of soluble fibre in the form of pectin. Eating apples with their skins offers the maximum amount of fibre. Research has shown that eating apples can also benefit the teeth as it appears to help to prevent gum disease.

Date and walnut flapjacks

Flapjacks are a favourite sweet for lunchboxes as well as for coffee or teatime. The modern streamlined version here uses less butter than usual, and adds dates for natural sweetness as well as walnuts and sunflower seeds for extra texture. The result is both nutritious and delicious.

Makes 16 flapjacks

100 g (3½ oz) unsalted butter

3 tbsp sunflower oil

55 g (2 oz) light muscovado sugar

3 tbsp clear honey

grated zest of 1 orange

2 tbsp orange juice

100 g (3½ oz) dried stoned dates, chopped

75 g (2½ oz) walnut pieces, chopped

250 g (8½ oz) porridge oats

30 g (1 oz) sunflower seeds

Preparation time: 15 minutes
Cooking time: 20 minutes

1 Preheat the oven to 180°C (350°F, gas mark 4). Lightly grease a shallow non-stick baking tin measuring 28 x 18 x 2.5 cm (11 x 7 x 1 in), or a 20 cm (8 in) square tin. If you do not have a non-stick tin, lightly grease an ordinary baking tin, then line the bottom with baking parchment.

2 Place the butter, oil, sugar, honey, and orange zest and juice in a heavy-based saucepan and heat gently, stirring until the butter has melted. Remove the pan from the heat and stir in the dates and walnuts. Then stir in the oats, making sure they are evenly coated with the butter mixture.

3 Turn the mixture into the prepared tin, pressing it down firmly and evenly. Sprinkle the sunflower seeds over the top and press down so they are lightly embedded in the surface.

4 Bake for 20 minutes or until deep golden around the edges. Remove from the oven and allow to cool slightly in the tin, then mark out 16 pieces on the top surface with a sharp knife.

5 Leave to cool completely, still in the tin, before cutting into bars along the marked lines. The flapjacks can be kept in an airtight container for up to 1 week.

Plus points

• Oats are an excellent source of soluble fibre, which can help to reduce high blood cholesterol levels.

• Up to 95% of the calorie content of dates comes from natural sugars, but because of their fibre content – and additional fibre from the oats in this recipe – the body can keep the release of glucose into the bloodstream at a steady pace, resulting in a gentle and sustained rise in blood sugar levels for long-term energy, rather a sudden rise for a quick energy fix and then a fast dip.

• Sunflower seeds are a rich source of vitamin E and also provide vitamin B_1, niacin and zinc.

Each flapjack provides Ⓥ

kcal 208, **protein** 3 g, **fat** 13 g (of which saturated fat 4 g), **carbohydrate** 22 g (of which sugars 11 g), **fibre** 2 g

✓✓✓ E

✓ B_1, copper, zinc

Some more ideas

- Sprinkle the top with pumpkin seeds instead of the sunflower seeds.
- Other dried fruits, such as dried cranberries or plump juicy raisins, can be added to the flapjack mixture, in addition to the dates, or add 2 tbsp good quality mincemeat.

- Substitute desiccated coconut for 30 g (1 oz) of the muscovado sugar.
- To make apricot and hazelnut flapjacks, substitute 100 g (3½ oz) chopped ready-to-eat dried apricots for the dates and 75 g (2½ oz) chopped toasted hazelnuts for the walnuts.
- For muesli and ginger flapjacks, make the

butter mixture as in the main recipe but use just 2 tbsp honey, and replace the orange zest and juice with 2 tbsp apple juice, 2 pieces of finely chopped preserved stem ginger and 1 tbsp ginger syrup from the jar. Stir in 340 g (12 oz) sugar-free muesli with dried fruits and nuts. Sprinkle with flaked almonds before baking.

Summer berry muffins

Fresh summer berries not only add delicious flavour and colour to these tempting American-style muffins, they also make them more nutritious. The muffins are at their best when served warm, fresh from the oven, but will be enjoyed just as much once cooled – an ideal addition to a lunchbox, or for breakfast on the go.

Makes 9 muffins

115 g (4 oz) plain wholemeal flour
85 g (3 oz) plain white flour
1 tbsp baking powder
pinch of salt
140 g (5 oz) mixed fresh berries, such as
   blueberries and raspberries
55 g (2 oz) butter
55 g (2 oz) light soft brown sugar
1 egg, beaten
200 ml (7 fl oz) semi-skimmed milk

Preparation time: 10 minutes
Cooking time: 20 minutes

Each muffin provides Ⓥ

kcal 166, **protein** 4 g, **fat** 6 g (of which
saturated fat 4 g), **carbohydrate** 24 g (of
which sugars 9 g), **fibre** 2 g

✓   A, E, calcium, selenium

1 Preheat the oven to 200°C (400°F, gas mark 6). Use paper muffin cases to line a 9-cup muffin tray – each cup should measure about 7 cm (scant 3 in) across the top and be about 3 cm (1¼ in) deep.

2 Sift the flours, baking powder and salt into a bowl, tipping in any bran left in the sieve. Gently fold in the mixed berries.

3 Melt the butter gently in a small saucepan, then add the sugar, egg and milk and mix until smooth. Pour this over the flour mixture and gently fold the ingredients together, just enough to combine them. The mixture should remain quite lumpy.

4 Spoon the mixture into the muffin cases, filling each about two-thirds full. Bake for 18–20 minutes or until the muffins are risen and golden brown.

5 Transfer to a wire rack to cool slightly, then serve warm or allow to cool completely before serving. The muffins can be kept in an airtight tin for 1–2 days.

Some more ideas

● Instead of a mixture of white and wholemeal flour, use all white or all wholemeal flour.
● For a hint of spice, add 1½ tsp ground mixed spice, ginger or cinnamon with the flour.
● Replace the berries with other fresh fruit, such as chopped apples, apricots, peaches or strawberries, or dried fruit, such as sultanas, raisins, chopped apricots, dates or figs.
● To make pear and cinnamon oatmeal muffins, mix 200 g (7 oz) self-raising wholemeal flour, 55 g (2 oz) medium oatmeal, 1 tsp baking powder, 1½ tsp ground cinnamon and a pinch of salt in a bowl. Fold in 2 peeled and chopped dessert pears. In a separate bowl, mix together 55 g (2 oz) melted butter, 55 g (2 oz) caster sugar, 2 eggs and 150 ml (5 fl oz) orange juice. Pour this over the flour mixture and fold the ingredients together. Spoon into 9 muffin cases and bake as in the main recipe.
● For mini muffins, divide the batter among 30 mini paper muffin cases and bake for 10 minutes.

Plus points

● Combining wholemeal flour with white flour increases the fibre content of these muffins and adds valuable nutrients such as B-group vitamins.
● Fresh berries are naturally low in fat. They offer dietary fibre and make a good contribution to vitamin C intake. Raspberries also supply vitamin E, and blueberries, like cranberries, contain a compound that helps to prevent urinary-tract infections.

Sticky prune and ginger teabread

The texture of this irresistible teabread is a mixture of crumbly ginger-spiced cake and a sticky, sweet prune purée that is rippled through it. The teabread keeps well – in fact, it improves after being stored for a day or two – and is a good choice for an energy-giving lunchbox sweet.

Makes 1 loaf, to cut into 12 slices

200 g (7 oz) ready-to-eat stoned prunes, coarsely chopped

100 ml (3½ fl oz) strong Earl Grey tea, cooled

115 g (4 oz) unsalted butter

75 g (2½ oz) light muscovado sugar

75 g (2½ oz) golden syrup

300 g (10½ oz) self-raising flour

½ tsp baking powder

½ tsp ground cinnamon

1 egg, beaten

6 tbsp semi-skimmed milk

75 g (2½ oz) stem ginger in syrup, drained and chopped

2 tsp stem ginger syrup (optional)

Preparation time: 30–35 minutes
Cooking time: 1–1¼ hours

Each slice provides ⓥ

kcal 240, **protein** 4 g, **fat** 9 g (of which saturated fat 5 g), **carbohydrate** 39 g (of which sugars 20 g), **fibre** 2 g

✓   A, E, calcium

1 Preheat the oven to 160°C (325°F, gas mark 3). Use baking parchment to line a large loaf tin measuring 23 x 13 x 6 cm (9 x 5 x 2½ in).

2 Place the prunes and tea in a small saucepan and bring to the boil. Reduce the heat, cover the pan and simmer gently for about 10 minutes or until almost all of the liquid has been absorbed by the prunes.

3 Tip the prunes into a food processor or blender and process to a fairly smooth purée. Set aside.

4 Place the butter, sugar and golden syrup in a saucepan and heat gently until just melted and smooth. Remove from the heat and cool slightly.

5 Sift the flour, baking powder and cinnamon into a large bowl and make a well in the centre. Add the warm syrup mixture, the egg and milk, and beat well to mix thoroughly. Reserve about 1 tbsp of the chopped ginger and stir the rest into the cake mixture.

6 Spoon about one-third of the cake mixture into the prepared tin and spread over the bottom. Top with about half the prune purée, spreading it into an even layer. Add another third of the cake mixture and spread out evenly, then spread the remaining prune purée over that. Finally, spoon the remaining cake mixture on top and smooth it out.

7 Sprinkle the reserved chopped ginger over the surface of the cake. Bake for 1–1¼ hours or until well risen, golden brown and firm to the touch. Cool in the tin for about 10 minutes, then turn out onto a wire rack and leave to cool completely.

8 Brush the top of the teabread with the stem ginger syrup, if using, then wrap in foil and store for at least 24 hours before slicing. The teabread will keep for up to a week.

Plus points

• Prunes provide useful amounts of iron, potassium and vitamin B_6. They are also a high fibre food, naturally low in sodium and virtually fat free. Independent of the dietary fibre content, prunes are known to have a laxative effect and can be helpful in treating constipation.

• Compared to other similar recipes, this teabread is a good choice for a healthy diet as it uses less sugar, due to the inclusion of naturally sweet prunes, and less fat.

Some more ideas

• Simmer the prunes in apple juice rather than Earl Grey tea.

• For a quicker version of this teabread, chop the prunes into small chunks and, instead of cooking them in the tea, simply stir them into the cake mixture with the ginger pieces. As this teabread will be less moist, reduce the baking time to about 1 hour.

• To make peach and orange teabread, replace the prunes with ready-to-eat dried peaches and simmer them in orange juice rather than tea. Reduce the quantity of ginger to 50 g (1¾ oz) and add it all to the cake mixture with the finely grated zest of 1 orange.

Fruit and pistachio baklava

Here is an updated version of the traditional Greek pastries, made with a cinnamon-spiced filling of dried dates, dried mango and pistachio nuts, layered with filo pastry. Although this baklava uses less fat and honey than usual, it is most definitely a special sweet snack and sure to be a winner.

Makes 20 squares

55 g (2 oz) butter

2 tbsp sunflower oil

85 g (3 oz) dried mango, finely chopped

85 g (3 oz) stoned dried dates, finely chopped

115 g (4 oz) pistachio nuts, finely chopped

1½ tsp ground cinnamon

8 tbsp clear honey

20 sheets filo pastry, about 18 x 30 cm (7 x 12 in) each

4 tbsp orange juice

Preparation time: 40 minutes
Cooking time: 20–25 minutes

Each square provides Ⓥ

kcal 196, **protein** 4 g, **fat** 10 g (of which saturated fat 2 g), **carbohydrate** 24 g (of which sugars 15 g), **fibre** 2 g

✓✓	E
✓	copper

1 Gently heat the butter and oil in a small saucepan until melted and blended. Remove the pan from the heat and set aside. Mix together the dried mango, dates, pistachios, cinnamon and 4 tbsp of the honey in a bowl. Set aside.

2 Preheat the oven to 220°C (425°F, gas mark 7). Lightly grease a shallow 18 x 28 cm (7 x 11 in) baking tin with a little of the melted butter and oil mixture.

3 Place one sheet of filo pastry in the bottom of the tin, allowing the pastry to come up the sides of the tin if necessary, and brush sparingly with the butter and oil mixture. Layer in 4 more sheets of filo, brushing each one lightly with the mix of oil and butter. Spread with one-third of the fruit mixture.

4 Repeat the layering of filo sheets and fruit mixture 2 more times. Top this final layer of fruit filling with the remaining 5 sheets of filo, brushing each with a little of the melted butter and oil. Trim the edges of the pastry to fit the tin.

5 Mark the surface of the top pastry layer into 20 squares using the tip of a sharp knife. Bake for 15 minutes, then reduce the oven temperature to 180°C (350°F, gas mark 4). Bake for a further 10–15 minutes or until the pastry is crisp and golden brown.

6 Meanwhile, gently warm the remaining 4 tbsp honey with the orange juice in a small saucepan until blended, stirring constantly.

7 When the pastry has finished baking, remove it from the oven and pour the honey and orange mixture evenly over the surface. Leave it to cool in the tin. When cold, cut into the marked squares for serving.

Plus points

• Filo pastry is a lower-fat alternative to shortcrust and puff pastries. In 100 g (3½ oz) of filo pastry there are 2 g fat and 275 kcals, whereas the same weight of shortcrust pastry contains 29 g fat and 449 kcals.

• The sweetness of fruit is concentrated in its dried form, so no additional sugar is needed in the filling for this pastry. Dried fruit is also a significant source of dietary fibre.

sweet treats

150

Some more ideas

● To make peach or apricot and pecan baklava, use 170 g (6 oz) chopped ready-to-eat dried peaches or apricots in place of the dates and mango, and chopped pecan nuts (or hazelnuts) in place of some or all of the pistachios. Spice with ground ginger, nutmeg or mixed spice instead of cinnamon.

● For pear, hazelnut and almond baklava, make the filling by mixing together 55 g (2 oz) finely chopped hazelnuts, 55 g (2 oz) finely chopped almonds, 85 g (3 oz) chopped ready-to-eat dried pears, 85 g (3 oz) sultanas, 1½ tsp ground mixed spice and the finely grated zest of 1 small lemon.

Fruit brochettes with rosewater cashew cream

Serving fresh fruit threaded on skewers is an attractive alternative to making a fruit salad and is a great way of pairing complementary fruit. It will entice children to eat more fruit, too. Here an exotic nut cream flavoured with rosewater transforms the simple combination of ripe apricots and cherries.

Serves 4

12 ripe apricots, about 300 g (10½ oz) in total

32 ripe sweet cherries, about 250 g (8½ oz) in total, stoned

Rosewater cashew cream

100 g (3½ oz) unsalted cashew nuts

120 ml (4 fl oz) apple juice

2 tsp rosewater

To decorate (optional)

1 tsp icing sugar

fresh mint leaves

Preparation time: about 20 minutes, plus at least 30 minutes chilling

Each serving provides Ⓥ

kcal 211, **protein** 6 g, **fat** 12 g (of which saturated fat 2 g), **carbohydrate** 21 g (of which sugars 17 g), **fibre** 3 g

✓✓✓	copper
✓✓	B₁, C
✓	B₆, E, folate, niacin, potassium

1 First prepare the rosewater cashew cream. Grind the cashew nuts in a food processor or blender to a fine powder, then continue grinding until it starts to clump together slightly. Alternatively, use a pestle and mortar to grind the nuts. Add 2 tbsp of the apple juice and grind again. Continue adding the apple juice a little at a time, grinding after each addition to ensure that the juice combines well with the nuts, to form a pale creamy mixture.

2 Stir the rosewater into the cashew and apple cream and transfer to 4 small pots or a serving dish. Cover and chill for at least 30 minutes. (It can be made up to a day ahead.)

3 Halve and stone the apricots, then cut them into wedges. Thread the apricots and cherries onto 8 wooden skewers. Place the skewers on plates, serving 2 per portion.

4 Put the icing sugar in a tea strainer and dust a little over the fruit brochettes. Decorate with fresh mint leaves and serve with the rosewater cashew cream.

Plus points

• Cherries were almost certainly grown in the orchards of Mesopotamia, but their cultivation in Europe is much more recent. They are a particularly good source of potassium. Eaten on a daily basis, they appear to help lower levels of uric acid and thus may reduce any risk of developing gout.

• A nut cream is a healthy alternative to dairy cream as a topping for desserts, because although nuts have a high fat content, the majority is the 'healthier' monounsaturated type.

• Apple juice provides good amounts of potassium, which, with sodium, is important for maintaining fluid balance, regulating blood pressure and keeping a healthy heart. Apple juice is also a good natural sweetener.

Some more ideas

● To serve the fruit brochettes hot, soak the skewers in warm water for 10 minutes before threading on the fruit. Place in a foil-lined grill pan and sprinkle with 1 tsp icing sugar. Cook under a preheated hot grill for about 3 minutes, then turn and sprinkle with another 1 tsp icing sugar. Grill for a further 2–3 minutes or until hot and lightly browned in places.

● Try other fruit pairings on the skewers, for example wedges of kiwi fruit with chunks of banana, chunks of Galia or Ogen melon with whole strawberries, or chunks of pineapple with halved ready-to-eat prunes.

● Serve the brochettes with orange and honey yogurt instead of the cashew cream. Mix 1 tsp orange-flower water and 2 tsp clear honey with 300 g (10½ oz) plain low-fat yogurt.

Mango smoothie

Smoothies are speedy and satisfying fruit drinks – as thick as a milk shake – that can either be made with milk and yogurt or just with pure fruit juices and fruit pulp. Almost any fresh fruit can be used, on its own or in combination. To serve more than 2, simply make a second batch of smoothies.

Serves 2

1 ripe mango
150 g (5½ oz) plain low-fat yogurt, chilled
300 ml (10 fl oz) semi-skimmed milk, chilled
1 tsp clear honey, or to taste
seeds from 6 cardamom pods

Preparation time: 5 minutes

1 Peel the skin off the mango and cut the flesh away from the stone. Chop the flesh roughly and place it in a blender or food processor. Process until smooth.

2 Pour in the yogurt and milk, and continue to process until well mixed and frothy. Sweeten with honey to taste.

3 Pour into 2 tall glasses and sprinkle the cardamom seeds over the top. Serve immediately.

Some more ideas

● For a tropical banana smoothie, replace the mango and plain yogurt with 1 large sliced banana and 150 g (5½ oz) low-fat, tropical fruit-flavoured yogurt.

● To make a kiwi and raspberry smoothie, use 2 peeled and chopped kiwi fruits, 225 g (8 oz) raspberries and 300 ml (10 fl oz) apple or white grape juice. Sweeten to taste with a little honey, if necessary.

● Try a pear and blackberry smoothie, made with 2 peeled, cored and chopped ripe dessert pears, 125 g (4½ oz) blackberries, the pulpy flesh of 2 passion fruit and 300 ml (10 fl oz) cranberry juice.

● Another delicious smoothie is pineapple and strawberry. Use 1 peeled, cored and chopped small pineapple with 225 g (8 oz) strawberries, 300 ml (10 fl oz) apple juice and 1 tbsp elderflower cordial.

Plus points

● Smoothies are made very quickly, using raw fruit, so they retain the maximum nutritional value of their ingredients.

● When made with milk and yogurt, a smoothie will also contain protein, calcium and many B vitamins – getting close to being a meal in a glass.

● Mango is an excellent source of the antioxidant beta-carotene, which the body can convert into vitamin A. This vitamin is essential for healthy skin and good vision, especially in dim light. Mangoes also provide substantial amounts of vitamin C as well as vitamins B_6 and E.

Each serving provides (V)

kcal 207, **protein** 10 g, **fat** 3 g (of which saturated fat 2 g), **carbohydrate** 37 g (of which sugars 37 g), **fibre** 4 g

✓✓✓	A, C, E
✓✓	B_2, B_6, B_{12}, calcium
✓	B_1, folate, niacin, copper, potassium, zinc

sweet treats

A glossary of nutritional terms

Antioxidants These are compounds that help to protect the body's cells against the damaging effects of free radicals. Vitamins C and E, beta-carotene (the plant form of vitamin A) and the mineral selenium, together with many of the phytochemicals found in fruit and vegetables, all act as antioxidants.

Calorie A unit used to measure the energy value of food and the intake and use of energy by the body. The scientific definition of 1 calorie is the amount of heat required to raise the temperature of 1 gram of water by 1 degree Centigrade. This is such a small amount that in this country we tend to use the term kilocalories (abbreviated to *kcal*), which is equivalent to 1000 calories. Energy values can also be measured in kilojoules (kJ): 1 kcal = 4.2 kJ.

A person's energy (calorie) requirement varies depending on his or her age, sex and level of activity. The estimated average daily energy requirements are:

Age (years)	Female (kcal)	Male (kcal)
1–3	1165	1230
4–6	1545	1715
7–10	1740	1970
11–14	1845	2220
15–18	2110	2755
19–49	1940	2550
50–59	1900	2550
60–64	1900	2380
65–74	1900	2330

Carbohydrates These energy-providing substances are present in varying amounts in different foods and are found in three main forms: sugars, starches and non-starch polysaccharides (NSP), usually called fibre.

There are two types of sugars: *intrinsic sugars*, which occur naturally in fruit (fructose) and sweet-tasting vegetables, and *extrinsic sugars*, which include lactose (from milk) and all the non-milk extrinsic sugars (NMEs) – sucrose (table sugar), honey, treacle, molasses and so on. The NMEs, or 'added' sugars, provide only calories, whereas foods containing intrinsic sugars also offer vitamins, minerals and fibre. Added sugars (*simple carbohydrates*) are digested and absorbed rapidly to provide energy very quickly. Starches and fibre (*complex carbohydrates*), on the other hand, break down more slowly to offer a longer-term energy source (see also Glycaemic Index). Starchy carbohydrates are found in bread, pasta, rice,

wholegrain and breakfast cereals, and potatoes and other starchy vegetables such as parsnips, sweet potatoes and yams.

Healthy eating guidelines recommend that at least half of our daily energy (calories) should come from carbohydrates, and that most of this should be from complex carbohydrates. No more than 11% of our total calorie intake should come from 'added' sugars. For an average woman aged 19–49 years, this would mean a total carbohydrate intake of 259 g per day, of which 202 g should be from starch and intrinsic sugars and no more than 57 g from added sugars. For a man of the same age, total carbohydrates each day should be about 340 g (265 g from starch and intrinsic sugars and 75 g from added sugars).

See also Fibre and Glycogen.

Cholesterol There are two types of cholesterol – the soft waxy substance called blood cholesterol, which is an integral part of human cell membranes, and dietary cholesterol, which is contained in food. *Blood cholesterol* is important in the formation of some hormones and it aids digestion. High blood cholesterol levels are known to be an important risk factor for coronary heart disease, but most of the cholesterol in our blood is made by the liver – only about 25% comes from cholesterol in food. So while it would seem that the amount of cholesterol-rich foods in the diet would have a direct effect on blood cholesterol levels, in fact the best way to reduce blood cholesterol is to eat less saturated fat and to increase intake of foods containing soluble fibre.

Fat Although a small amount of fat is essential for good health, most people consume far too much. Healthy eating guidelines recommend that no more than 33% of our daily energy intake (calories) should come from fat. Each gram of fat contains 9 kcal, more than twice as many calories as carbohydrate or protein, so for a woman aged 19–49 years this means a daily maximum of 71 g fat, and for a man in the same age range 93.5 g fat.

Fats can be divided into 3 main groups: saturated, monounsaturated and polyunsaturated, depending on the chemical structure of the fatty acids they contain. *Saturated fatty acids* are found mainly in animal fats such as butter and other dairy products and in fatty meat. A high intake of saturated fat is known to be a risk factor for coronary heart disease and certain types of cancer. Current guidelines are that no more than 10% of our daily calories should come from saturated fats, which is about 21.5 g for an adult woman and 28.5 g for a man.

Where saturated fats tend to be solid at room temperature, the *unsaturated fatty acids* –

monounsaturated and polyunsaturated – tend to be liquid. *Monounsaturated fats* are found predominantly in olive oil, groundnut (peanut) oil, rapeseed oil and avocados. Foods high in *polyunsaturates* include most vegetable oils – the exceptions are palm oil and coconut oil, both of which are saturated.

Both saturated and monounsaturated fatty acids can be made by the body, but certain polyunsaturated fatty acids – known as *essential fatty acids* – must be supplied by food. There are 2 'families' of these essential fatty acids: *omega-6*, derived from linoleic acid, and *omega-3*, from linolenic acid. The main food sources of the omega-6 family are vegetable oils such as olive and sunflower; omega-3 fatty acids are provided by oily fish, nuts, and vegetable oils such as soya and rapeseed.

When vegetable oils are hydrogenated (hardened) to make margarine and reduced-fat spreads, their unsaturated fatty acids can be changed into trans fatty acids, or '*trans fats*'. These artificially produced trans fats are believed to act in the same way as saturated fats within the body – with the same risks to health. Current healthy eating guidelines suggest that no more than 2% of our daily calories should come from trans fats, which is about 4.3 g for an adult woman and 5.6 g for a man. In thinking about the amount of trans fats you consume, remember that major sources are processed foods such as biscuits, pies, cakes and crisps.

Fibre Technically non-starch polysaccharides (NSP), fibre is the term commonly used to describe several different compounds, such as pectin, hemicellulose, lignin and gums, which are found in the cell walls of all plants. The body cannot digest fibre, nor does it have much nutritional value, but it plays an important role in helping us to stay healthy.

Fibre can be divided into 2 groups – soluble and insoluble. Both types are provided by most plant foods, but some foods are particularly good sources of one type or the other. *Soluble fibre* (in oats, pulses, fruit and vegetables) can help to reduce high blood cholesterol levels and to control blood sugar levels by slowing down the absorption of sugar. *Insoluble fibre* (in wholegrain cereals, pulses, fruit and vegetables) increases stool bulk and speeds the passage of waste material through the body. In this way it helps to prevent constipation, haemorrhoids and diverticular disease, and may protect against bowel cancer.

Our current intake of fibre is around 12 g a day. Healthy eating guidelines suggest that we need to increase this amount to 18 g a day.

Free radicals These highly reactive molecules can cause damage to cell walls and DNA (the genetic material found within cells). They are believed to be involved in the development of heart disease, some cancers and premature ageing. Free radicals are produced naturally by the body in the course of everyday life, but certain factors, such as cigarette smoke, pollution and over-exposure to sunlight, can accelerate their production.

Gluten A protein found in wheat and, to a lesser degree, in rye, barley and oats, but not in corn (maize) or rice. People with *coeliac disease* have a sensitivity to gluten and need to eliminate all gluten-containing foods, such as bread, pasta, cakes and biscuits, from their diet.

Glycaemic Index (GI) This is used to measure the rate at which carbohydrate foods are digested and converted into sugar (glucose) to raise blood sugar levels and provide energy. Foods with a high GI are quickly broken down and offer an immediate energy fix, while those with a lower GI are absorbed more slowly, making you feel full for longer and helping to keep blood sugar levels constant. High-GI foods include table sugar, honey, mashed potatoes and watermelon. Low-GI foods include pulses, wholewheat cereals, apples, cherries, dried apricots, pasta and oats.

Glycogen This is one of the 2 forms in which energy from carbohydrates is made available for use by the body (the other is *glucose*). Whereas glucose is converted quickly from carbohydrates and made available in the blood for a fast energy fix, glycogen is stored in the liver and muscles to fuel longer-term energy needs. When the body has used up its immediate supply of glucose, the stored glycogen is broken down into glucose to continue supplying energy.

Minerals These inorganic substances perform a wide range of vital functions in the body. The *macrominerals* – calcium, chloride, magnesium, potassium, phosphorus and sodium – are needed in relatively large quantities, whereas much smaller amounts are required of the remainder, called *microminerals*. Some microminerals (selenium, magnesium and iodine, for example) are needed in such tiny amounts that they are known as *'trace elements'*.

There are important differences in the body's ability to absorb minerals from different foods, and this can be affected by the presence of other substances. For example, oxalic acid, present in spinach, interferes with the absorption of much of the iron and calcium spinach contains.
• *Calcium* is essential for the development of strong bones and teeth. It also plays an important role in blood clotting. Good sources include dairy products, canned fish (eaten with their bones) and dark green, leafy vegetables.
• *Chloride* helps to maintain the body's fluid balance. The main source in the diet is table salt.
• *Chromium* is important in the regulation of blood sugar levels, as well as levels of fat and cholesterol in the blood. Good dietary sources include red meat, liver, eggs, seafood, cheese and wholegrain cereals.

• *Copper*, component of many enzymes, is needed for bone growth and the formation of connective tissue. It helps the body to absorb iron from food. Good sources include offal, shellfish, mushrooms, cocoa, nuts and seeds.
• *Iodine* is an important component of the thyroid hormones, which govern the rate and efficiency at which food is converted into energy. Good sources include seafood, seaweed and vegetables (depending on the iodine content of the soil in which they are grown).
• *Iron* is an essential component of haemoglobin, the pigment in red blood cells that carries oxygen around the body. Good sources are offal, red meat, dried apricots and prunes, and iron-fortified breakfast cereals.
• *Magnesium* is important for healthy bones, the release of energy from food, and nerve and muscle function. Good sources include wholegrain cereals, peas and other green vegetables, pulses, dried fruit and nuts.
• *Manganese* is a vital component of several enzymes that are involved in energy production and many other functions. Good dietary sources include nuts, cereals, brown rice, pulses and wholemeal bread.
• *Molybdenum* is an essential component of several enzymes, including those involved in the production of DNA. Good sources are offal, yeast, pulses, wholegrain cereals and green leafy vegetables.
• *Phosphorus* is important for healthy bones and teeth and for the release of energy from foods. It is found in most foods. Particularly good sources include dairy products, red meat, poultry, fish and eggs.
• *Potassium*, along with sodium, is important in maintaining fluid balance and regulating blood pressure, and is essential for the transmission of nerve impulses. Good sources include fruit, especially bananas and citrus fruits, nuts, seeds, potatoes and pulses.
• *Selenium* is a powerful antioxidant that protects cells against damage by free radicals. Good dietary sources are meat, fish, dairy foods, brazil nuts, avocados and lentils.
• *Sodium* works with potassium to regulate fluid balance, and is essential for nerve and muscle function. Only a little sodium is needed – we tend to get too much in our diet. The main source in the diet is table salt, as well as salty processed foods and ready-prepared foods.
• *Sulphur* is a component of 2 essential amino acids. Protein foods are the main source.
• *Zinc* is vital for normal growth, as well as reproduction and immunity. Good dietary sources include oysters, red meat, peanuts and sunflower seeds.

Phytochemicals These biologically active compounds, found in most plant foods, are believed to be beneficial in disease prevention. There are literally thousands of different phytochemicals, amongst which are the following:

• *Allicin*, a phytochemical found in garlic, onions, leeks, chives and shallots, is believed to help lower high blood cholesterol levels and stimulate the immune system.
• *Bioflavonoids*, of which there are at least 6000, are found mainly in fruit and sweet-tasting vegetables. Different bioflavonoids have different roles – some are antioxidants, while others act as anti-disease agents. A sub-group of these phytochemicals, called *flavonols*, includes the antioxidant *quercetin*, which is believed to reduce the risk of heart disease and help to protect against cataracts. Quercetin is found in tea, red wine, grapes and broad beans.
• *Carotenoids*, the best known of which are *beta-carotene* and *lycopene*, are powerful antioxidants thought to help protect us against certain types of cancer. Highly coloured fruits and vegetables, such as blackcurrants, mangoes, tomatoes, carrots, sweet potatoes, pumpkin and dark green, leafy vegetables, are excellent sources of carotenoids.
• *Coumarins* are believed to help protect against cancer by inhibiting the formation of tumours. Oranges are a rich source.
• *Glucosinolates*, found mainly in cruciferous vegetables, particularly broccoli, Brussels sprouts, cabbage, kale and cauliflower, are believed to have strong anti-cancer effects. *Sulphoraphane* is one of the powerful cancer-fighting substances produced by glucosinolates.
• *Phytoestrogens* have a chemical structure similar to the female hormone oestrogen, and they are believed to help protect against hormone-related cancers such as breast and prostate cancer. One of the types of these phytochemicals, called *isoflavones*, may also help to relieve symptoms associated with the menopause. Soya beans and chickpeas are a particularly rich source of isoflavones.

Protein This nutrient, necessary for growth and development, for maintenance and repair of cells, and for the production of enzymes, antibodies and hormones, is essential to keep the body working efficiently. Protein is made up of *amino acids*, which are compounds containing the 4 elements that are necessary for life: carbon, hydrogen, oxygen and nitrogen. We need all of the 20 amino acids commonly found in plant and animal proteins. The human body can make 12 of these, but the remaining 8 – called *essential amino acids* – must be obtained from the food we eat.

Protein comes in a wide variety of foods. Meat, fish, dairy products, eggs and soya beans contain all of the essential amino acids, and are therefore called first-class protein foods. Pulses, nuts, seeds and cereals are also good sources of protein, but do not contain the full range of essential amino acids. In practical terms, this really doesn't matter – as long as you include a variety of different protein foods in your diet, your body will get all the amino acids it needs. It is important, though, to eat protein foods every day because the essential amino acids cannot be stored in the body for later use.

The RNI of protein for women aged 19–49 years is 45 g per day and for men of the same age 55 g. In the UK most people eat more protein than they need, although this isn't normally a problem.

Reference Nutrient Intake (RNI) This denotes the average daily amount of vitamins and minerals thought to be sufficient to meet the nutritional needs of almost all individuals within the population. The figures, published by the Department of Health, vary depending on age, sex and specific nutritional needs such as pregnancy. RNIs are equivalent to what used to be called Recommended Daily Amounts or Allowances (RDA).

RNIs for adults (19–49 years)

Vitamin A	600–700 mcg
Vitamin B_1	0.8 mg for women, 1 mg for men
Vitamin B_2	1.1 mg for women, 1.3 mg for men
Niacin	13 mg for women, 17 mg for men
Vitamin B_6	1.2 mg for women, 1.4 mg for men
Vitamin B_{12}	1.5 mg
Folate	200 mcg (400 mcg for first trimester of pregnancy)
Vitamin C	40 mg
Vitamin E	no recommendation in the UK; the EC RDA is 10 mg, which has been used in all recipe analyses in this book
Calcium	700 mg
Chloride	2500 mg
Copper	1.2 mg
Iodine	140 mcg
Iron	14.8 mg for women, 8.7 mg for men
Magnesium	270–300 mg
Phosphorus	550 mg
Potassium	3500 mg
Selenium	60 mcg for women, 75 mcg for men
Sodium	1600 mg
Zinc	7 mg for women, 9.5 mg for men

Vitamins These are organic compounds that are essential for good health. Although they are required in only small amounts, each one has specific vital functions to perform. Most vitamins cannot be made by the human body, and therefore must be obtained from the diet. The body is capable of storing some vitamins (A, D, E, K and B_{12}), but the rest need to be provided by the diet on a regular basis. A well-balanced diet, containing a wide variety of different foods, is the best way to ensure that you get all the vitamins you need.

Vitamins can be divided into 2 groups: *water-soluble* (B complex and C) and *fat-soluble* (A, D, E and K). Water-soluble vitamins are easily destroyed during processing, storage, and the preparation and cooking of food. The fat-soluble vitamins are less vulnerable to losses during cooking and processing.

• *Vitamin A* (retinol) is essential for healthy vision, eyes, skin and growth. Good sources include dairy products, offal (especially liver), eggs and oily fish. Vitamin A can also be obtained from *beta-carotene*, the pigment found in highly coloured fruit and vegetables. In addition to acting as a source of vitamin A, beta-carotene has an important role to play as an antioxidant in its own right.

• *The B Complex vitamins* have very similar roles to play in nutrition, and many of them occur together in the same foods.

Vitamin B_1 (thiamin) is essential in the release of energy from carbohydrates. Good sources include milk, offal, meat (especially pork), wholegrain and fortified breakfast cereals, nuts and pulses, yeast extract and wheat germ. White flour and bread are fortified with B_1 in the UK.

Vitamin B_2 (riboflavin) is vital for growth, healthy skin and eyes, and the release of energy from food. Good sources include milk, meat, offal, eggs, cheese, fortified breakfast cereals, yeast extract and green leafy vegetables.

Niacin (nicotinic acid), sometimes called vitamin B_3, plays an important role in the release of energy within the cells. Unlike the other B vitamins it can be made by the body from the essential amino acid tryptophan. Good sources include meat, offal, fish, fortified breakfast cereals and pulses. White flour and bread are fortified with niacin in the UK.

Pantothenic acid, sometimes called vitamin B_5, is involved in a number of metabolic reactions, including energy production. This vitamin is present in most foods; notable exceptions are fat, oil and sugar. Good sources include liver, kidneys, yeast, egg yolks, fish roe, wheat germ, nuts, pulses and fresh vegetables.

Vitamin B_6 (pyridoxine) helps the body to utilise protein and contributes to the formation of haemoglobin for red blood cells. B_6 is found in a wide range of foods including meat, liver, fish, eggs, wholegrain cereals, some vegetables, pulses, brown rice, nuts and yeast extract.

Vitamin B_{12} (cyanocobalamin) is vital for growth, the formation of red blood cells and maintenance of a healthy nervous system. B_{12} is unique in that it is principally found in foods of animal origin. Vegetarians who eat dairy products will get enough, but vegans need to ensure they include food fortified with B_{12} in their diet. Good sources of B_{12} include liver, kidneys, oily fish, meat, cheese, eggs and milk.

Folate (folic acid) is involved in the manufacture of amino acids and in the production of red blood cells. Recent research suggests that folate may also help to protect against heart disease. Good sources of folate are green leafy vegetables, liver, pulses, eggs, wholegrain cereal products and fortified breakfast cereals, brewers' yeast, wheatgerm, nuts and fruit, especially grapefruit and oranges.

Biotin is needed for various metabolic reactions and the release of energy from foods. Good sources include liver, oily fish, brewers' yeast, kidneys, egg yolks and brown rice.

• *Vitamin C* (ascorbic acid) is essential for growth and vital for the formation of collagen (a protein needed for healthy bones, teeth, gums, blood capillaries and all connective tissue). It plays an important role in the healing of wounds and fractures, and acts as a powerful antioxidant. Vitamin C is found mainly in fruit and vegetables.

• *Vitamin D* (cholecalciferol) is essential for growth and the absorption of calcium, and thus for the formation of healthy bones. It is also involved in maintaining a healthy nervous system. The amount of vitamin D occurring naturally in foods is small, and it is found in very few foods – good sources are oily fish (and fish liver oil supplements), eggs and liver, as well as breakfast cereals, margarine and full-fat milk that are fortified with vitamin D. Most vitamin D, however, does not come from the diet but is made by the body when the skin is exposed to sunlight.

• *Vitamin E* is not one vitamin, but a number of related compounds called tocopherols that function as antioxidants. Good sources of vitamin E are vegetable oils, polyunsaturated margarines, wheatgerm, sunflower seeds, nuts, oily fish, eggs, wholegrain cereals, avocados and spinach.

• *Vitamin K* is essential for the production of several proteins, including prothombin which is involved in the clotting of blood. It has been found to exist in 3 forms, one of which is obtained from food while the other 2 are made by the bacteria in the intestine. Vitamin K_1, which is the form found in food, is present in broccoli, cabbage, spinach, milk, margarine, vegetable oils, particularly soya oil, cereals, liver, alfalfa and kelp.

Nutritional analyses

The nutritional analysis of each recipe has been carried out using data from *The Composition of Foods* with additional data from food manufacturers where appropriate. Because the level and availability of different nutrients can vary, depending on factors like growing conditions and breed of animal, the figures are intended as an approximate guide only.

The analyses include vitamins A, B_1, B_2, B_6, B_{12}, niacin, folate, C, D and E, and the minerals calcium, copper, iron, potassium, selenium and zinc. Other vitamins and minerals are not included, as deficiencies are rare. Optional ingredients and optional serving suggestions have not been included in the calculations.

glossary

Index

Titles in italics are for recipes in 'Some more ideas'.

A

Afternoon tea 24–5
Allicin 68, 157
Almond polenta biscuits 138
Anchovies: Egg and anchovy pan bagna 68
  Pissaladière 124–5
Antioxidants 156
Apples: Apple and hazelnut drop scones 143
  Pork and apple sloppy Joes 62
  Smoked mackerel and apple open sandwiches 70
Apricots: *Apricot and hazelnut flapjacks* 145
  Fruit brochettes with rosewater cashew cream 152–3
Aubergines: *Aubergine and mozzarella bruschetta* 53
  Baked rigatoni with aubergine 102–3
  Middle Eastern aubergine purée 31
Avocados: *Guacamole topping* 37

B

Bacon and pineapple pizza muffins 50
Baklava: Fruit and pistachio baklava 150–1
  Peach and pecan baklava 151
Bananas: Caramelised banana crumpets 140
  Tropical banana smoothie 154
Beans: Fennel and bean salad 76
  Mixed bean patties with sweetcorn relish 67
Beef: Sloppy Joes 62
Beetroot: Vegetable crisps 32–3
Beta-carotene 38, 41, 44, 64, 70, 72, 81, 154
Bioflavonoids 78, 157
Biscuits: *Almond polenta biscuits* 138
  Blue cheese and walnut biscuits 134
  Orange and pecan biscuits 138

Bread, sandwiches 18–19
Breakfast 20
Bruschetta, Chorizo, grilled pepper and tomato 52–3

C

Calcium 50, 58, 61, 64, 68, 70, 78, 86, 88, 105, 106, 118, 124, 129, 130, 134, 140, 154, 157
Calories 156
Cannellini beans: *Pepper and cannellini bean salad* 76
  Tuscan bean crostini 28
Caramelised banana crumpets 40
Caramelised onion tartlets 116
Carbohydrates 6, 57, 84, 94, 100, 156
Carotenoids 157
Carrots: Sardine, watercress and carrot open sandwich 70
Cashew nut cream 152–3
Cheese: *Aubergine and mozzarella bruschetta* 53
  Blue cheese and walnut biscuits 134
  Cheese and onion rarebit 61
  Cheese and tomato rarebit 61
  Cheese and watercress soufflé 105
  Goat's cheese toasts 129
  Gorgonzola and pear rarebit 61
  Greek-style salad loaf 68
  Mushroom and thyme toasts 58
  Nachos 34
  Sardine, watercress and carrot open sandwich 70
  Sesame cheese twists 134
  Sugarsnap salad with black grapes and feta cheese 78
Cherries: Fruit brochettes with rosewater cashew cream 152–3
Chicken: Chicken and cashew pancakes 98–9
  Chicken yakitori 126
  Hoisin chicken wraps 72
  Oriental chicken salad 83
  Tarragon chicken salad 82–3
  Tropical chicken rice 100
Chickpeas: Falafel pittas 67
  Pitta crisps with hummus 30–1
Children's parties 25
Chilli and herb dip 39
Chloride 157
Cholesterol 42, 116, 144, 156
Chorizo, grilled pepper and tomato bruschetta 52–3

Chromium 157
Clams: *New England clam chowder* 87
Cod: Fish dim sum 120–1
Copper 110, 116, 122, 129, 157
Coumarins 157
Courgettes: Potato and courgette tortilla 42
Couscous: Spiced couscous tomatoes 84–5
Crab: Gingered crab filo parcels 112–13
  Piquant crab dip with crudités 41
Crisps, vegetable 32–3
Crostini, Tuscan bean 28
Crudités, Piquant crab dip with 41
Crumpets, caramelised banana 140

D

Dairy foods 6
Date and walnut flapjacks 144–5
Dim sum, fish 120–1
Dinner parties 24
Dips: *Chilli and herb* 39
  Creamy mustard 38–9
  Piquant crab 41
  Smoked mackerel 41
Dried fruit: Spiced fruits, nuts and seeds 44
Drinks 14
Drop scones, Apple and hazelnut 143
Duck: *Sesame duck pancakes* 99

E

Eggs: Egg and anchovy pan bagna 68
  Mushroom and herb omelette 90–1
  Potato and courgette tortilla 42
  Potato, mushroom and Parmesan tortilla 42
  Scrambled egg and ham rolls 55
  Spinach omelette with Parma ham crisps 91
  Tomato and basil soufflé omelette 91

F

Falafel pittas 67
Fat 7, 156
Fennel and bean salad 76
Fibre 28, 30, 36, 44, 54, 78, 84, 98, 102, 106, 134, 143, 144, 146, 148, 150, 156
Finger food 22–3, 109–35

Fish dim sum 120–1
Flageolet beans: Fennel and bean salad 76
Flapjacks, Date and walnut 144–5
Folate 32, 64, 76, 92, 158
Free radicals 156–7
Fruit 6
  Summer berry muffins 146
  Fruit and pistachio baklava 150–1

G

Garlic mushroom rolls 55
Gingered crab filo parcels 112–13
Glucosinolates 157
Gluten 157
Glycaemic Index (GI) 15, 157
Glycogen 157
Goat's cheese toasts 129
Gorgonzola and pear rarebit 61
Grapes: Sugarsnap salad with black grapes and feta cheese 78
Greek meatballs with lemon dip 132–3
Greek-style salad loaf 68
Guacamole topping 37

H

Ham: Leek and ham pizza muffins 50
Hazelnuts: Apple and hazelnut drop scones 143
Herring roes, mustard fried 57
Hoisin chicken wraps 72
Hummus, Pitta crisps with 30–1

I, J

Iodine 96, 110, 120, 130, 157
Iron 54, 62, 67, 70, 84, 88, 90, 92, 98, 110, 118, 124, 129, 134, 148, 157
Japanese soup noodles with smoked tofu and bean sprouts 88

K, L

Kiwi and raspberry smoothie 154
Lamb: Greek meatballs with lemon dip 132–3
Leek and ham pizza muffins 50
Lentil risotto 106
Lunch 10, 16–21, 75–107
Lycopene 81, 124

M

Magnesium 98, 129, 134, 157
Manganese 157

Mangoes: Mango and tomato salsa 34
  Mango smoothie 154
Meatballs, Greek 132–3
Mediterranean-style vegetable salad with sardine toasts 81
Middle Eastern salad 81
Milk: Mango smoothie 154
Minerals 157
Mini spring rolls 113
Molybdenum 157
Monkfish and mussel sticks 110
Muesli and ginger flapjacks 145
Muffins: Leek and ham pizza muffins 50
  Summer berry muffins 146
Mushrooms: *Devilled mushroom toasts* 58
  Garlic mushroom rolls 55
  Lentil risotto 106
  Mushroom and carrot sushi
  Mushroom and herb omelette 90–1
  Mushroom and spinach pasta bake 103
  Mushroom and thyme toasts 58
  Mushroom and tofu dim sum 121
  Mushrooms stuffed with spring greens and walnuts 122
  Mushrooms with red pepper and pine nut filling 122
  Potato, mushroom and Parmesan tortilla 42
  Stuffed mushrooms 122
Mussels: Monkfish and mussel sticks 110
Mustard: Creamy mustard dip 38–9
  Mustard fried herring roes 57

N

Nachos 34
Nectarine brioche fingers 140
New England clam chowder 87
Niacin 42, 90, 124, 129, 144, 158
Noodles: Japanese soup noodles with smoked tofu and bean sprouts 88
  Thai noodles with prawns and lemongrass 88
  Vegetable stir-fry with rice noodles 93
Nuts: Spiced fruits, nuts and seeds 44

O

Oats: Date and walnut flapjacks 144–5
Olives, Rosemary marinated 47
Omega-3 fatty acids 36, 70, 72
Omelettes: Mushroom and herb 90–1
Spinach with Parma ham crisps 91
Tomato and basil soufflé omelette 91
Onions: Caramelised onion tartlets 116
Cheese and onion rarebit 61
Orange and pecan biscuits 138
Oriental chicken salad 83
Oriental spare ribs 115

P

Packed lunches 18–21
Pak choy: Stir-fry pork with Chinese greens 92–3
Pan bagna, egg and anchovy 68
Pancakes: Chicken and cashew 98–9
Sesame duck 99
Party food 22–5, 109–35
Pasta: Baked rigatoni with aubergine 102–3
Peaches: *Fresh peach salsa 34*
Peach and orange teabread 149
Peach and pecan baklava 151
Peanut dip 32–3
Pearl barley 'risotto' 106
Pears: *Gorgonzola and pear rarebit 61*
Pear and blackberry smoothie 154
Pear and cinnamon oatmeal muffins 146
Pear, grape and spinach salad 78
Pear, hazelnut and almond baklava 151
Pecan nuts: Orange and pecan biscuits 138
Peppers: Chorizo, grilled pepper and tomato bruschetta 52–3
Nachos 34
Pepper and cannellini bean salad 76
Rosemary marinated olives 47
Phosphorus 41, 64, 68, 78, 86, 92, 110, 129, 157
Phytochemicals 61, 157

Phytoestrogens 76, 157
Pineapple: *Bacon and pineapple pizza muffins 50*
Pineapple and Black Forest bites 118
Pineapple and strawberry smoothie 154
Pissaladière 124–5
Pistachio nuts: Fruit and pistachio baklava 150–1
Pitta breads: Falafel pittas 67
Middle Eastern salad 81
Pitta crisps with hummus 30–1
Pork: *Pork and apple sloppy Joes 62*
Sticky spare ribs 115
Stir-fry pork with Chinese greens 92–3
Potassium 41, 76, 86, 110, 129, 130, 140, 148, 152, 157
Potatoes: Baked potato skins with smoked salmon and fresh dill 36–7
Home-style potato cakes with baked beef tomatoes 94–5
Potato and courgette tortilla 42
Potato, mushroom and Parmesan tortilla 42
Rosti-style potato and spinach cakes 95
Smoked haddock hash 96
Vegetable crisps with peanut dip 32–3
Prawns: *Prawn filo parcels 113*
Prawn sushi 130
Scallop and prawn sticks 110
Thai coconut rice with prawns 100
Thai noodles with prawns and lemongrass 88
Tomato and ginger prawns on toast 57
Tomatoes filled with prawns and cottage cheese 85
Protein 7, 58, 67, 78, 82, 88, 96, 100, 154, 157–8
Prunes: Sticky prune and ginger teabread 148–9

R

Ratatouille tartlets 116
Reference Nutrient Intake (RNI) 158
Rice: Sushi rolls 130
Thai coconut rice with prawns 100
Tropical chicken rice 100

Rigatoni with aubergine 102–3
Risotto, lentil 106
Rosemary marinated olives 47
Rosti-style potato and spinach cakes 95

S

Salads: Fennel and bean salad 76
Mediterranean-style vegetable salad with sardine toasts 81
Middle Eastern salad 81
Oriental chicken salad 83
Pear, grape and spinach salad 78
Pepper and cannellini bean salad 76
Sugarsnap salad with black grapes and feta cheese 78
Tarragon chicken salad 82–3
Salmon: Grilled salmon in ciabatta 64
Salmon and tomato chowder 86–7
Salmon and tomato topping 37
Salmon yakitori 126
Salsa, mango and tomato 34
Sandwiches 18–19
Sardines: *Mediterranean-style vegetable salad with sardine toasts 81*
Sardine, watercress and carrot open sandwich 70
Scallop and prawn sticks 110
Seeds, Spiced fruits, nuts and 44
Selenium 86, 98, 100, 116, 134, 157
Sesame cheese twists 134
Sloppy Joes 62
Smoked haddock: *Smoked haddock and spinach soufflé 105*
Smoked haddock hash 96
Smoked mackerel: *Smoked mackerel and apple open sandwiches 70*
Smoked mackerel dip 41
Smoked salmon: Baked potato skins with 36–7
Sushi rolls 130
Smoked trout wraps 72
Snacks 10, 12–14
Sodium 148, 152, 157
Soufflé, Cheese and watercress 105
Soups: Japanese soup noodles with smoked tofu and bean sprouts 88

New England clam chowder 87
Salmon and tomato chowder 86–7
Sweetcorn and blue cheese chowder 87
Spare ribs, sticky 115
Spinach omelette with Parma ham crisps 91
Sugarsnap salad with black grapes and feta cheese 78
Sulphur 157
Summer berry muffins 146
Sushi rolls 130
Sweetcorn: *Mixed bean patties with sweetcorn relish 67*
Sweetcorn and blue cheese chowder 87
Swordfish sticks 110

T

Tapenade goat's cheese toasts 129
Taramasalata: Smoked trout wraps 72
Tarragon chicken salad 82–3
Tartlets, Caramelised onion 116
Teabread, Sticky prune and ginger 148–9
Tex Mex-style sloppy Joes 62
Thai coconut rice with prawns 100
Thai noodles with prawns and lemongrass 88
Tofu: Japanese soup noodles with smoked tofu and bean sprouts 88
Tomatoes: Chorizo, grilled pepper and tomato bruschetta 52–3
Home-style potato cakes with baked beef tomatoes 94–5
Mango and tomato salsa 34
Pissaladière 124–5
Salmon and tomato chowder 86–7
Sloppy Joes 62
Spiced couscous tomatoes 84–5
Spicy tomato dip 33
Tomato and basil soufflé omelette 91
Tomato and ginger prawns on toast 57
Tomato and ham pizza muffins 50
Tomato and pancetta pissaladière 125
Tomato and red pepper pissaladière 125

Tomatoes filled with prawns and cottage cheese 85
Tortilla: Potato and courgette 42
Potato, mushroom and Parmesan 42
Tortillas: Smoked trout wraps 72
Tortilla chips with fresh mango and tomato salsa 34
Tuna: *Grilled tuna baps 64*
Hot and spicy tuna rolls 54–5
Middle Eastern salad 81
Tuna crostini 28
Tuna sticks 110
Turkey: Smoked turkey and apricot bites 118
Turkey and sage meatballs 133
Tuscan bean crostini 28

V

Vegetables 6
Spiced root vegetable wedges with creamy mustard dip 38–9
Vegetable crisps with peanut dip 32–3
Vegetable stir-fry with rice noodles 93
Vitamin A 38, 47, 57, 90, 130, 154, 158
Vitamin B 42, 52, 57, 58, 62, 64, 78, 82, 86, 88, 90, 92, 100, 102, 106, 110, 122, 124, 129, 130, 134, 144, 146, 148, 154, 158
Vitamin C 34, 54, 57, 78, 81, 84, 94, 96, 100, 146, 154, 158
Vitamin D 57, 158
Vitamin E 44, 50, 57, 72, 78, 90, 96, 116, 122, 134, 138, 144, 154, 158
Vitamin K 158

W

Watercress: Cheese and watercress soufflé 105
Sardine, watercress and carrot open sandwich 70

Z

Zinc 44, 62, 90, 92, 105, 110, 116, 129, 134, 144, 157

*Printing and binding: Printer Industria Gráfica S.A.,Barcelona
Separations:Colour Systems Ltd, London
Paper: Condat, France*

index